POETRY OF THE AMERICAN WEST

Other Columbia University Press Reference books:

The Columbia Book of Civil War Poetry
Edited by Richard Marius

The Columbia Anthology of American Poetry
Edited by Jay Parini

The Columbia Anthology of British Poetry
Edited by Carl Woodring and James Shapiro

The Columbia History of American Poetry
Edited by Jay Parini

The Columbia History of British Poetry
Edited by Carl Woodring and James Shapiro

The Columbia History of the American Novel
Edited by Emory Elliot

The Columbia Literary History of the United States
Edited by Emory Elliot

POETRY OF THE AMERICAN WEST

A Columbia Anthology

Edited by ALISON HAWTHORNE DEMING

COLUMBIA UNIVERSITY PRESS ✳ *New York*

COLUMBIA UNIVERSITY PRESS

NEW YORK   CHICHESTER, WEST SUSSEX

A list of permissions may be found on pages 00–000.

All photographs courtesy of the National Archives, unless otherwise noted.

Library of Congress Cataloging-in-Publication Data
Poetry of the American West / edited by Alison Hawthorne Deming
    p. cm.
  Includes bibliographical references and index.
  ISBN 0–231–10386–7 (alk. paper)
  1. American Poetry—West (U.S.) 2. West (U.S.)—Poetry.
I. Deming, Alison Hawthorne.
PS561.P58   1996
811.008'03278—dc20   95–40648
                                    CIP

CONTENTS ✳

To experience the American West is to be moved by the power and beauty of the land—from the rosy rimrock of Utah's Canyonlands to the forested flanks of the Rockies and Cascades; from the flowering starkland of the Mojave and Sonoran Deserts to the hardworking Pacific that shapes California's elegant coast. But for the scrupulous contemporary observer, no American landscape can be seen without also seeing the history of people's relationship with the land and with one another. Historically, the western landscape, characterized by its open space and aridity, has exacted a price from those who would know it. And it has been inhabited by a particularly brutal history of cultural collisions.

I undertook the project of this anthology in order to find out what the poetry of the American West had to contribute to our understanding of that history. In considering the project, I found no current anthology of western poetry that offered a sufficient breadth of inquiry. Though many fine ones have been published in recent years, they tend to be narrowly committed to a single regional or cultural perspective—anthologies of Montana, Oregon, or Nevada poets, American Indian or Latino poets , cowboy and ranch women poets. All fine projects, making valuable contributions by highlighting specific strengths and directions in poetry. Yet none offered an integrated vision of poetry of the West, none worked toward creating a communal sense of western poetics that might include regional, aesthetic, and cultural difference. By taking a thematic focus as my editorial bias, I have worked with the intention of crossing regional, aesthetic, and cultural borders. I should add that I have favored *American Indian* throughout the anthology as the generic term of choice for the native tribal people of what is now the United States. Though this term is too general to encompass the rich and diverse tribal heritage of our continent, and though it derives from the mistaken apprehension of early European explorers that they had landed in India, nevertheless *American Indian*, or simply *Indian*, is currently the term in most common usage among both scholars of the West and tribal people.

The anthologist's first problem is that of definition. What is the West? Where and when does it begin? To Philip Freneau, writing in New York in the 1700s, it was Ohio; Willa Cather's frontier was situated in Nebraska; to Lorna Dee Cervantes and Adrienne Rich the freeways and depleted croplands of California define the western frontier. The definition of the West changes over time. It is both the place and the process of people immigrating to that place. The West is a construction of easterners. If you live in Mexico, "the West" is actually to the north; if you live in Canada, "the West" is to the south. To keep myself within somewhat fixed boundaries, I chose to work with the geography from the one-hundredth meridian to the West coast, from the Mexican border to the Canadian border. Those borders, particularly the U.S.–Mexico border, have been fixed in their present locations for a relatively short time, historically speaking. I crossed the border to include Nahuatl flower songs from the Aztec world of ancient Mexico—technically not "American poetry," yet providing a poetic remnant of the great cultural flowering whose influence radiated into what we know as the American Southwest.

This raised the question of defining the very idea of a "western poetic tradition." The antecedents to contemporary western poetry are broad and varied and represent not merely different cultures and regions, but different functions. The sacred songs of the Aztecs, the epic poems of Gaspar Pérez de Villagrá and John Neihardt, the protest poems of the Chicano farmworkers' movement, the meditations of Theodore Roethke, cowboy songs traded around the campfire, and the imagistic Romantic lyrics of Robert Hass and Joy Harjo may differ dramatically in form and intended function. Yet in theme they have in common the need to give shape and meaning to one's experience of the land and the land's authority.

Rather than being definitive, then, this anthology is intended to be impressionistic—a poet's reading of the fluid traditions and directions of poetry of the American West. Beyond the general thematic consideration, my editorial taste has been guided by several principles. I have wanted the anthology to offer a broad aesthetic range including genteel verse, tribal song, political and protest poems, balladry, populist poems such as cowboy songs and corridos, and work championing both traditional and exploratory literary forms. I have wanted to represent the new democracy in American poetry; I believe we are hearing more good poems from a wider cultural range of the American people than ever in history. The current flourishing of American Indian and Latino writing, for example, is unprecedented. Where such new voices will lead the art, I do not know. But clearly, they will lead it somewhere, not merely follow what has been done before. I have wanted to hear what some of our best poets have had to say about the West and their relationship with it; and I have wanted to place those poems in conversation with one another. I have therefore omitted many bland and familiar chestnuts of popular western poetry, in favor of work with a more serious literary intent or of a distinctive and quirky voice.

And I have worked to select a group of poems that will serve the reader in two ways. First, as a reference book, this collection provides many points of access for those seeking a path into the unfamiliar terrain of western poetry. Second, as a whole, the anthology tells a story about the West that I believe is instructive for our present predicament. We know that the old story of the West—the story of manifest destiny, of westering when the land we've lived on becomes too crowded or tainted with our mistakes, of rugged individualism against harsh circumstance and savage foes—is dead. The world has grown smaller than it was when that story was told, the trees fewer, the water table lower, and the western population larger and increasingly more international. The great dangers of the wild rarely feel so dangerous to us any longer. In fact, we long for our own wildness, as John Daniel and David Wagoner remind us, and for the spiritual lessons wilderness can teach. The life that early westerners fought so hard for—the one that meant taking a living out of the land as rancher, miner, or logger—is eroding with the rootless soil on clear-cut hillsides and is being replaced by the equally rootless life of tourism and recreational industry. We feel the sorry moral consequences of our ancestors' deeds as a burden, not a heroic legacy. Everywhere we look, in the wilds and in the city, the land is stained with human blood. The new story of the West is just beginning to be written—part elegy to the past, part rage at its injustices; part imaginative retelling of the past so that we understand how our collective character has been formed, part the good American optimism in the ideal of freedom—freedom earned not at the cost of communal well-being, but in its service.

ACKNOWLEDGMENTS ✳

Behind this book stands a community of friends and colleagues without whom I could not have persevered. For research assistance and moral support in the often daunting task of gathering these poems, I thank Brendon MacBryde, Keith Frome, Karen Falkenstrom, Richard Shelton, Judy Temple, and Colleen Burns. For thinking and writing about the American West in a way that expanded my thinking, I thank William Kittredge, Gary Paul Nabhan, Wallace Stegner (in memoriam), Benjamin Alire Sáenz, and Terry Tempest Williams. I thank Jennifer McDonald and James Raimes for working out the details. And, with apology if I appear self-serving, I thank the University of Arizona Poetry Center for providing an exceptional collection of poetry books and a wide open space in which to explore them.

POETRY OF THE AMERICAN WEST

Nahuatl Flower Songs

The first known poems of America are the Nahuatl flower songs, or cuicamatl *(papers of song), of the Aztec people. Collected by sixteenth-century Spanish friars, some of these poems predate the Conquest.*

NEZAHUALCOYOTL (1402–1472) ✳

Nezahualcoyotl of Tezcoco, a poet and leader, oversaw the construction of roads and aqueducts, palaces and ceremonial halls, in addition to composing sacred songs.[1]

Flower Songs

My flowers will not come to an end,
my songs will not come to an end,
I, the singer, raise them up;
they are scattered, they are bestowed . . .
Even though flowers on earth
may wither and yellow,
they will be carried there,
to the interior of the house
of the bird with the golden feathers.

✳

With flowers You paint,
O Giver of Life!
With songs You give color,
with songs You shade
those who will live on the earth.
Later you will destroy eagles and tigers:
we live only in Your painting
here, on the earth.
With black ink You will blot out

2

all that was friendship,
brotherhood, nobility.

You give shading
to those who will live on the earth.
We live only in Your book of paintings,
here, on the earth.

✴

I comprehend the secret, the hidden:
O my lords!
Thus we are,
we are mortal,
human through and through,
we all will have to go away,
we all will have to die on earth . . .
Like a painting,
we will be erased.
Like a flower,
we will dry up
here on earth.
Like plumed vestments of the precious bird,
that precious bird with the agile neck,
we will come to an end . . .
Think on this, o lords,
eagles and tigers,
though you be of jade,
though you be of gold,
you also will go there,
to the place of the fleshless.
We will have to disappear,
no one can remain.

In a festival lasting several days, the Aztecs prayed for rain, paying for the anticipated gift with the sacrifice of small children, whose weeping would serve as an omen of heavy rain. The prayers and songs of this ritual drama, excerpted here, were recorded and translated into Spanish by Friar Bernadino de Sahagún in the sixteenth century.[2]

Song for the Festival of Tlaloc, the Rain God

PRIEST:
Now it is time for you to weep!
Alas, I was created
and for my god
festal bundles of blood-stained ears of corn
I carry now
to the divine hearth

You are my chief, Prince Magician,

and though in truth

it is you who produce our sustenance,

though you are the first,

only you cause us shame.

In all of this there is no Tlaloc.

If anyone

is filled with shame,

it is because he did not know me well;

and as my father, by my priesthood,

Serpents and Tigers.

CHOIR IN THE VOICE OF THE CHILD:
I will go away forever,
it is time for crying.
Send me to the Place of Mystery,
under your command.
I have already told
the Prince of the Sad Omen,
I will go away forever,
it is time for crying.
In four years
comes the arising among us,
many people
without knowing it;
in the place of the fleshless,
the house of quetzal feathers,
is the transformation.
It is the act of the Propagator of Men.

PRIEST:
Go to all parts,
spread out
in Poyauhtlan,
in the region of mist.
With timbrels of mist
our word is carried to Tlalocan.

CACAMATZIN (1494–1520) ✳

Cacamatzin, the grandson of Nezahualcoyotl, was the last king of Tezcoco, a ruler and poet who had a brief and tragic life. Both his father, Nezahualpilli, and his grandfather had been warriors, rulers, and composers of songs. Cacamatzin recorded the arrival of "strange foreigners who brought with them weapons that spit forth fire and animals so high that they were taller than deer." He later suffered imprisonment and torture by the Spanish, and in song he called on the power of the elders.[3]

My Friends

My friends,
listen to this:
let no one live deluded with a pretension of royalty.
The fury, the clashes,
let them be forgotten,
disappear
in due time from the earth.

Also, to me alone,
a short time ago they said,
those who were at the ball court,
they said, they murmured:
Is it possible to work mercifully?
Is it possible to act prudently?
I know only myself.
Everyone says this,
but no one speaks truly on earth.

The mist spreads,
the conch shells resound
over me and over all the earth.
Flowers rain down, they interweave, whirl about,
they come to bring joy upon the earth.

It is truly, perhaps as in His House,
our Father acts,
perhaps like quetzal plumage in springtime,
with flowers he paints,
here on the earth, the Giver of Life.
In the place where the precious drums play,
where are heard the beautiful flutes,
of the precious God, Lord of the heavens,
necklaces of red feathers
tremble over the earth.

A mist wraps round the song of the shields,
over the earth falls a rain of darts,
they darken the color of all the flowers,
there is noise of thunder in the heavens.
With shields of gold
there they dance.

I only say,
I Cacamatzin,
now alone I remember
Lord Nezahualpilli.
Perhaps they speak there,
he and Nezahualcoyotl,
in the place of the drums?
I remember them now.

Truly who will not have to go there?
If he is jade, if he is gold,
perhaps he will not have to go there?

Am I perchance a shield of turquoise,
will I as a mosaic be embedded once more in existence?
Will I come again to the earth?
Will I be shrouded in fine mantles?
Still on earth, near the place of the drums,
I remember them.

NAHUATL (SIXTEENTH CENTURY) ✳ *Among the testimonies about the Conquest recorded in song by the Aztecs is this* icnocuítcatl *(elegy, or sad song), not attributed to an individual poet.*[4]

Elegy

And all this happened to us.
We saw it,
we marveled at it.
With this sad and mournful destiny
we saw ourselves afflicted.
On the roads lie broken arrows,
our hair is in disarray.
Without roofs are the houses,
and red are their walls with blood.
Worms multiply in the streets and squares,
and on the walls brains are spattered.
Red are the waters, as if they were dyed,
and when we drink,
it seems water of saltpeter.
We have struggled against the walls of adobe,
but our heritage was a net made of holes.

Our shields were our protection
but not even with shields could we defend ourselves.
We have eaten branches of linnet,
we have chewed upon salty witch grass,
bits of adobe and ground earth,
small lizards, rats, worms. . . .
We ate meat
when it was scarcely on the fire.
When the meat was cooked,
we snatched it out of
the very coals and ate it.
They put a price on us.
The price for a young person, for a priest,
a child or a young girl.
And it was enough: for a common man
the price was only two handfuls of corn
or ten portions of caked mosquitoes,
our price was only
twenty portions of salty witch grass.
Gold, jade, rich mantles,
plumage of quetzal,
all that has value
was then counted as nothing. . . .

(Translated from the Spanish by Miguel Léon-Portilla and Grace Lobanov)

GASPAR PÉREZ DE VILLAGRÁ (C. 1555–1620) ✳

Villagrá was born at Puebla de Los Angeles in New Spain, probably in 1555, and returned to Spain to receive a degree from the University of Salamanca. He returned to New Spain sometime before 1596, when he enlisted in the colonizing expedition to New Mexico led by Don Juan de Oñate, one of the last territorial expansions of the Spanish Empire. The experience served as the basis for Villagrá's epic poem, the opening passages of which echo Virgil's Aeneid. *His* Historia *was first published in 1610. It preceded Captain John Smith's* General History of Virginia, *making it one of the earliest literary works addressing the European colonization of what is now the United States.*[5]

from History of New Mexico

from CANTO XVI

The world has no such pleasing joy
As may compare to that received
By the folk of a battered fleet
When, beaten by uproarious winds,
It takes a safe and pleasant port
In peaceful and well-known shelter.
Not otherwise all this your camp
At the end of adventures and events
And times of sorrow, misadventures, too,
Happy and in great pleasure did arrive
At a fine pueblo, well laid out,
To which they gave the title of San Juan
And "de los caballeros" to recall
The ones who first did elevate
In these new lands and regions
The bloody standard on which Christ
For general salvation was raised up.
Here all the Indians with pleasure
Did share their houses with our folk.
And when, all lodged and settled down,
We were endeavoring to be good neighbors,

Buffalo grazing, Wichita National Forest, Oklahoma, 1908.

Hoping that surely water would be given
For which they wept and grieved so much.
Now hardly another day gone by
To the hour of that weeping when the heavens,
Being covered o'er with clouds, poured down
So much water on all that land
That the barbarians were amazed
At the mercy the Lord had shown us there.

from CANTO XVII
After this all did travel on
Further into plains and found
Such sum and mighty herds of beasts
That 'twas a frightful thing to imagine them.
In size they are like Spanish bulls,
Wooly in the extreme and all humpbacked,
Of plenteous flesh and of black horns,
Most splendid lard and rich in fat,
And, like to he-goats, they have beards,
And they are so swift turning
They do run much more than deer,
And so many do go in bands
That twenty, thirty thousand head at once
Are often and commonly found.
And they enjoy such widespread plains
That for six or eight hundred leagues
All seems to be a peaceful sea
With no sort of valley or hill
Where a man can in any way
Limit his vision or rest it
Upon as much height as an orange occupies,
If such excess may so be said.

The General being at his meal one day,
The barbarians set up a wail
So loud and fearful that we thought
The last moment had now arrived
To the tremendous judgment, final point
Of universal end for all the world.
Wherefore, all being much perturbed,
Confused, we asked the translators
The cause of that wailing, and they replied
That 'twas for water all the people wept,
For much time now had passed away
In which the clouds had never watered
The earth, which, in a thousand places dry,
Was so cracked and so burnt with thirst
That 'twas impossible to raise
As much as one of the crops they had sown.
For this reason the Commissary, then,
And Father Fray Cristóbal, trusting in
The highest Good through which we live,
Did order that it should be cried aloud
That they should weep no more nor be downcast,
Because they would ask their Father,
Who there in Heaven was, to have pity
On all that land, and that they hoped,
Though these were disobedient children,
He yet would give much water to them all
And they would come in such good time
That all the planting might be saved.
And just as tender babes are quieted
When once assured of the things
For which they weep and grieve and tire themselves,
So they, all silent, were at peace,

And it is true, lord, to such an extent
That if by evil chance a man were lost
Upon these plains 'twould be the same
As though he were lost and did find himself
In the midst of the sea, beyond all hope
Of ever seeing himself freed from the strait.

(Translated from the Spanish by Miguel Encinias, Alfred Rodríguez, and Joseph P. Sánchez)

PHILIP FRENEAU (1752–1832) ✳ *Of French Huguenot descent, Freneau was born in New York and lived there much of his life. He worked as a teacher, a postal clerk, commandeer of a privateering brig, secretary to a planter in the West Indies, translating clerk for the State Department, and an editor, printer, and bookseller. He wrote patriotic and satirical verse, his first major verse collection,* The Poems of Philip Freneau, *appearing in 1786.*[6]

On the Civilization of the Western Aboriginal Country

Strange to behold, unmingled with surprize,
Old heights extinguished, and new heights arise,
Nature, herself, assume a different face,—
Yet such has been, and such will be the case.
Thus, in the concave of the heavens around,
Old stars, have vanished, and new stars been found,
Some stars, worn out, have ceased to shine or burn,
And some, relumed, to their old posts return.

Two wheels has Nature constantly in play,
She turns them both, but turns a different way;
What one creates, subsists a year, an hour,
Then, by destruction's wheel is crushed once more.
No art, no strength this wheel of fate restrains,
While matter, deathless matter, still remains,
Again, perhaps, new modelled, to revive,
Again to perish, and again to live!

THOU, who shalt rove the trackless western waste,
Tribes to reform, or have new *breeds* embraced,
Be but sincere!—the native of the wild
If wrong, is only Nature's ruder child;
The arts you teach, perhaps not ALL amiss,
Are arts destructive of domestic bliss,
The *Indian world*, on Nature's bounty cast,
Heed not the future, nor regard the past.—
They live—and at the evening hour can say,
We claim no more, for we have had our day.
The *Indian* native, taught the ploughman's art,
Still drives his oxen, with an *Indian* heart,
Stops when they stop, reclines upon the *beam*,
While briny sorrows from his eye-lids stream,
To think the ancient trees, that round him grow,
That shaded *wigwams* centuries ago
Must now descend, each venerated bough,
To blaze on fields where nature reign'd 'till now.

Of different mind, he sees not with your sight,
Perfect, perhaps, as viewed by Nature's light:
By Nature's dictates all his views are bent,
No more *imperfect* than his AUTHOR meant.

All moral virtue, joined in one vast frame,
In 'forms though varying, still endures the same;
Draws to one point, finds but one general end,
As bodies to one common centre tend.

Whether the impulse of the mind commands
To change a *creed*, or speculate in lands,
No matter which—with pain I see YOU go
Where wild *Missouri's* turbid waters flow,
There to behold, where simple Nature reign'd,
A thousand *Vices* for one *Virtue* gained;
Forests destroyed by *Helots*, and by slaves,
And forests cleared, to breed a race of knaves.—
The bare idea clouds the soul with gloom—
Better return, and plough the soil at home.

But, if devoid of subterfuge, or art,
You act from mere sincerity of heart,
If honor's ardor in the bosom glows
Nor *selfish* motives on *yourselves* impose,
Go, and convince the natives of the west
That *christian* morals are the first, the best;
And yet *the same* that beam'd thro' every age,
Adorn the *ancient*, or the modern page;
That, without which, no social compacts bind,
Nor *honor* stamps her image on mankind.

Go, teach what Reason dictates should be taught,
And learn from *Indians* one great Truth you ought,
That, though the world, wherever man exists,
Involved in darkness, or obscured in mists,
The *Negro*, scorching on *Angola's* coasts,
Or *Tartar*, shivering in *Siberian* frosts;
Take all, through all, through nation, tribe, or clan,
The child of Nature is the *better* man.

WILLIAM CULLEN BRYANT (1794–1878) ✳

Bryant began publishing poems at the age of thirteen. At age twenty he wrote his most important poems, "To a Waterfowl" and "Thanatopsis." He had a law practice in Great Barrington, Massachusetts, but gave up that career to pursue a literary life. In 1832 he traveled to Illinois (then considered, by easterners, "the West"), where he toured the prairie and ancient Indian burial mounds.[7]

The Prairies

These are the gardens of the Desert, these
The unshorn fields, boundless and beautiful,
For which the speech of England has no name—
The Prairies. I behold them for the first,
And my heart swells, while the dilated sight
Takes in the encircling vastness. Lo! they stretch,
In airy undulations, far away,
As if the ocean, in his gentlest swell,
Stood still, with all his rounded billows fixed,
And motionless forever.—Motionless?—

No—they are all unchained again. The clouds
Sweep over with their shadows, and, beneath,
The surface rolls and fluctuates to the eye;
Dark hollows seem to glide along and chase
The sunny ridges. Breezes of the South!
Who toss the golden and the flamelike flowers,
And pass the prairie-hawk that, poised on high,
Flaps his broad wings, yet moves not—ye have played
Among the palms of Mexico and vines
Of Texas, and have crisped the limpid brooks
That from the fountains of Sonora glide
Into the calm Pacific—have ye fanned
A nobler or a lovelier scene than this?
Man hath no power in all this glorious work:
The hand that built the firmament hath heaved
And smoothed these verdant swells, and sown their slopes
With herbage, planted them with island groves,
And hedged them round with forests. Fitting floor
For this magnificent temple of the sky—
With flowers whose glory and whose multitude
Rival the constellations! The great heavens
Seem to stoop down upon the scene in love,—
A nearer vault, and of a tenderer blue,
Than that which bends above our eastern hills.

　　As o'er the verdant waste I guide my steed,
Among the high rank grass that sweeps his sides
The hollow beating of his footstep seems
A sacrilegious sound. I think of those
Upon whose rest he tramples. Are they here—
The dead of other days?—and did the dust
Of these fair solitudes once stir with life

And burn with passion? Let the mighty mounds
That overlook the rivers, or that rise
In the dim forest crowded with old oaks,
Answer. A race, that long has passed away,
Built them;—a disciplined and populous race
Heaped, with long toil, the earth, while yet the Greek
Was hewing the Pentelicus to forms
Of symmetry, and rearing on its rock
The glittering Parthenon. These ample fields
Nourished their harvests, here their herds were fed,
When haply by their stalls the bison lowed,
And bowed his manéd shoulder to the yoke.
All day this desert murmured with their toils,
Till twilight blushed, and lovers walked, and wooed
In a forgotten language, and old tunes,
From instruments of unremembered form,
Gave the soft winds a voice. The red man came—
The roaming hunter tribes, warlike and fierce,
And the mound-builders vanished from the earth.
The solitude of centuries untold
Has settled where they dwelt. The prairie-wolf
Hunts in their meadows, and his fresh-dug den
Yawns by my path. The gopher mines the ground
Where stood their swarming cities. All is gone;
All—save the piles of earth that hold their bones,
The platforms where they worshipped unknown gods,
The barriers which they builded from the soil
To keep the foe at bay—till o'er the walls
The wild beleaguerers broke, and, one by one,
The strongholds of the plain were forced, and heaped
With corpses. The brown vultures of the wood
Flocked to those vast uncovered sepulchres,

And sat unscared and silent at their feast.
Haply some solitary fugitive,
Lurking in marsh and forest, till the sense
Of desolation and of fear became
Bitterer than death, yielded himself to die.
Man's better nature triumphed then. Kind words
Welcomed and soothed him; the rude conquerors
Seated the captive with their chiefs; he chose
A bride among their maidens, and at length
Seemed to forget—yet ne'er forgot—the wife
Of his first love, and her sweet little ones,
Butchered, amid their shrieks, with all his race.

    Thus change the forms of being. Thus arise
Races of living things, glorious in strength,
And perish, as the quickening breath of God
Fills them, or is withdrawn. The red man, too,
Has left the blooming wilds he ranged so long,
And, nearer to the Rocky Mountains, sought
A wilder hunting-ground. The beaver builds
No longer by these streams, but far away,
On waters whose blue surface ne'er gave back
The white man's face—among Missouri's springs,
And pools whose issues swell the Oregon—
He rears his little Venice. In these plains
The bison feeds no more. Twice twenty leagues
Beyond remotest smoke of hunter's camp,
Roams the majestic brute, in herds that shake
The earth with thundering steps—yet here I meet
His ancient footprints stamped beside the pool.

Still this great solitude is quick with life.
Myriads of insects, gaudy as the flowers
They flutter over, gentle quadrupeds,
And birds, that scarce have learned the fear of man,
Are here, and sliding reptiles of the ground,
Startlingly beautiful. The graceful deer
Bounds to the wood at my approach. The bee,
A more adventurous colonist than man,
With whom he came across the eastern deep,
Fills the savannas with his murmurings,
And hides his sweets, as in the golden age,
Within the hollow oak. I listen long
To his domestic hum, and think I hear
The sound of that advancing multitude
Which soon shall fill these deserts. From the ground
Comes up the laugh of children, the soft voice
Of maidens, and the sweet and solemn hymn
Of Sabbath worshippers. The low of herds
Blends with the rustling of the heavy grain
Over the dark brown furrows. All at once
A fresher wind sweeps by, and breaks my dream,
And I am in the wilderness alone.

* *Born in Massachusetts, Snow moved at age two with her family to Ohio and joined the Mormon religion when Joseph Smith arrived in the region. She became "Zion's Poetess," celebrating her faith in poems, many of which are still sung in Latter-day Saint congregations. Journeying to Missouri, then Illinois, and finally Utah in the forced migration of the Mormons, she became a wife in plural marriage to Brigham Young, as well as a prominent leader of Mormon women. She published two books of poetry, a biography, and instructional works.*[8]

Song of the Desert

Beneath the cloud-topp'd mountain,
    Beside the craggy bluff,
Where every dint of nature
Is rude and wild enough;
    Upon the verdant meadow,
Upon the sunburnt plain,
    Upon the sandy hillock;
We waken music's strain.

Beneath the pine's thick branches,
    That has for ages stood;
Beneath the humble cedar,
    And the green cotton-wood;
Beside the broad, smooth river,
    Beside the flowing spring,
Beside the limpid streamlet;
    We often sit and sing.

Bristlecone pine,
Inyo National Forest,
California, 1965.
PHOTO: LELAND J. PATER

Beneath the sparkling concave,
    When stars in millions come
To cheer the pilgrim strangers,
    And bid us feel at home;
Beneath the lovely moonlight,
    When Cynthia spreads her rays;
In social groups assembled,
    We join in songs of praise.

Cheer'd by the blaze of firelight,
    When twilight shadows fall,
And when the darkness gathers
    Around our spacious hall,
With all the warm emotion
    To saintly bosoms given,
In strains of pure devotion
    We praise the God of heaven.

WALT WHITMAN (1819–1892) ✳

Whitman, America's most influential poet, was born on Long Island, New York, and worked as a printer, teacher, journalist, and carpenter. In 1855 he self-published Leaves of Grass, *then a collection of twelve poems including what he would later title "Song of Myself." Emerson was one of the few who championed Whitman's poetry from the start. In 1865, after nursing men wounded in the Civil War, he was appointed to a position in the Department of the Interior, but he was fired shortly thereafter for the alleged immorality of his poems. He traveled to the West in 1879–1880.*[9]

Pioneers! O Pioneers!

     Come my tan-faced children,
Follow well in order, get your weapons ready,
Have you your pistols? have you your sharp-edged axes?
     Pioneers! O pioneers!

     For we cannot tarry here,
We must march my darlings, we must bear the brunt of danger,
We the youthful sinewy races, all the rest on us depend,
     Pioneers! O pioneers!

     O you youths, Western youths,
So impatient, full of action, full of manly pride and friendship,
Plain I see you Western youths, see you tramping with the foremost,
     Pioneers! O pioneers!

     Have the elder races halted?
Do they droop and end their lesson, wearied over there beyond the seas?
We take up the task eternal, and the burden and the lesson,
     Pioneers! O pioneers!

All the past we leave behind,
We debouch upon a newer mightier world, varied world,
Fresh and strong the world we seize, world of labor and the march,
      Pioneers! O pioneers!

We detachments steady throwing,
Down the edges, through the passes, up the mountain steep.
Conquering, holding, daring, venturing as we go the unknown ways.
      Pioneers! O pioneers!

We primeval forests felling,
We the rivers stemming, vexing we and piercing deep the mines within,
We the surface broad surveying, we the virgin soil upheaving,
      Pioneers! O pioneers!

Colorado men are we,
From the peaks gigantic, from the great sierras and the high plateaus,
From the mine and from the gully, from the hunting trail we come,
      Pioneers! O pioneers!

From Nebraska, from Arkansas,
Central inland race are we, from Missouri, with the continental blood intervein'd,
All the hands of comrades clasping, all the Southern, all the Northern,
      Pioneers! O pioneers!

O resistless restless race!
O beloved race in all! O my breast aches with tender love for all!
O I mourn and yet exult, I am rapt with love for all,
      Pioneers! O pioneers!

Raise the mighty mother mistress,
Waving high the delicate mistress, over all the starry mistress,
(bend your heads all,)
Raise the fang'd and warlike mistress, stern, impassive, weapon'd mistress,
Pioneers! O pioneers!

See my children, resolute children,
By those swarms upon our rear we must never yield or falter,
Ages back in ghostly millions frowning there behind us urging,
Pioneers! O Pioneers!

On and on the compact ranks,
With accessions ever waiting, with the places of the dead quick fill'd,
Through the battle, through defeat, moving yet and never stopping,
Pioneers! O pioneers!

O to die advancing on!
Are there some of us to droop and die? has the hour come?
Then upon the march we fittest die, soon and sure the gap is fill'd,
Pioneers! O pioneers!

All the pulses of the world,
Falling in they beat for us, with the Western movement beat,
Holding single or together, steady moving to the front, all for us,
Pioneers! O pioneers!

Life's involv'd and varied pageants,
All the forms and shows, all the workmen at their work,
All the seamen and the landsmen, all the masters with their slaves,
Pioneers! O Pioneers!

Line at the Land Office, Perry, Oklahoma, 1893.

All the hapless silent lovers,
All the prisoners in the prisons, all the righteous and the wicked,
All the joyous, all the sorrowing, all the living, all the dying,
      Pioneers! O pioneers!

I too with my soul and body,
We, a curious trio, picking, wandering on our way,
Through these shores amid the shadows, with the apparitions pressing,
      Pioneers! O pioneers!

Lo, the darting bowling orb!
Lo, the brother orbs around, all the clustering suns and planets,
All the dazzling days, all the mystic nights with dreams,
      Pioneers! O pioneers!

These are of us, they are with us,
All for primal needed work, while the followers there in embryo wait behind,
We to-day's procession heading, we the route for travel clearing,
      Pioneers! O pioneers!

O you daughters of the West!
O you young and elder daughters! O you mothers and you wives!
Never must you be divided, in our ranks you move united,
      Pioneers! O pioneers!

Minstrels latent on the prairies!
(Shrouded bards of other lands, you may rest, you have done your work,)
Soon I hear you coming warbling, soon you rise and tramp amid us,
      Pioneers! O pioneers!

Not for delectations sweet,
Not the cushion and the slipper, not the peaceful and the studious,
Not the riches safe and palling, not for us the tame enjoyment,
Pioneers! O pioneers!

Do the feasters gluttonous feast?
Do the corpulent sleepers sleep? have they lock'd and bolted doors?
Still be ours the diet hard, and the blanket on the ground,
Pioneers! O pioneers!

Has the night descended?
Was the road of late so toilsome? did we stop discouraged nodding on our way?
Yet a padding hour I yield you in your tracks to pause oblivious,
Pioneers! O pioneers!

Till the sound of trumpet,
Far, far off the daybreak call—hark! how loud and clear I hear it wind,
Swift! to the head of the army!—swift! spring to your places,
Pioneers! O pioneers!

The Prairie-Grass Dividing

The prairie-grass dividing—its own odor breathing,
I demand of it the spiritual corresponding,
Demand the most copious and close companionship of men,
Demand the blades to rise of words, acts, beings,
Those of the open atmosphere, coarse, sunlit, fresh, nutritious,
Those that go their own gait, erect, stepping with freedom and command—leading, not following,
Those with a never-quell'd audacity—those with sweet and lusty flesh, clear
of taint, choice and chary of its love-power,
Those that look carelessly in the faces of Presidents and Governors, as to say, *Who are you?*
Those of earth-born passion, simple, never constrained, never obedient,
Those of inland America.

Night on the Prairies

Night on the Prairies,
The supper is over, the fire on the ground burns low,
The wearied emigrants sleep, wrapt in their blankets;
I walk by myself—I stand and look at the stars, which I think now I never realized before.

Now I absorb immortality and peace,
I admire death and test propositions.

How plenteous! How spiritual! How resumé!
The same Old Man and Soul—the same old aspirations, and the same content.

I was thinking the day most splendid, till I saw what the not-day exhibited,
I was thinking this globe enough, till there sprang out so noiseless around me myriads of other globes.

Moored schooner, San Francisco, California, 1900.

Now while the great thoughts of space and eternity fill me, I will measure myself by them,
And now touch'd with the lives of other globes, arrived as far along as those of the earth,
Or waiting to arrive, or pass'd on farther than those of the earth,
I henceforth no more ignore them than I ignore my own life,
Or the lives on the earth arrived as far as mine, or waiting to arrive.

O I see now that life cannot exhibit all to me—as the day cannot,
I see that I am to wait for what will be exhibited by death.

Facing West from California's Shores

Facing west from California's shores,
Inquiring, tireless, seeking what is yet unfound,
I, a child, very old, over waves, towards the house of maternity, the land of migrations, look afar,
Look off the shores of my Western sea, the circle almost circled;
For starting westward from Hindustan, from the vales of Kashmere,
From Asia, from the north, from the God, the sage, and the hero,
From the south, from the flowery peninsulas and the spice islands,
Long having wander'd since, round the earth having wander'd,
Now I face home again, very pleas'd and joyous,
(But where is what I started for so long ago?
And why is it yet unfound?)

JOHN ROLLIN RIDGE (YELLOW BIRD, 1827–1867) ✴

Born in the Cherokee Nation east of Mississippi to a
Cherokee father and a white mother, Ridge was called
by his grandfather Chees-quat-a-law-ny, or Yellow Bird.
In 1839 his grandfather and father were murdered by
Cherokees in retaliation for their role in the loss of the
tribal homeland to the whites. Ridge was educated
briefly in Massachusetts, later in a missionary school in
Arkansas, where he studied Latin and Greek. In 1849
Ridge killed a Cherokee who allegedly had attacked
him as a result of old family grievances. He fled to
California in the gold rush, working as a miner and
trader, then as a journalist publishing articles and
poems under the name Yellow Bird.[10]

A Cherokee Love Song

Oh come with me by moonlight, love,
    And let us seek the river's shore;
My light canoe awaits thee, love,
    The sweetest burden e'er it bore!

The soft, low winds are whispering there,
    Of human beauty, human love,
And with approving faces, too,
    The stars are shining from above.

Come place thy small white hand in mine,
    My boat is 'neath those willow trees,
And with my practised arm, the oar
    Will ask no favor from the breeze.

Now, now we're on the waters, love,
    Alone upon the murmuring tide—
Alone! but why should we regret,
    If there were none on earth beside?

What matters it, if all were gone?
    Thy bird-like voice could yet beguile,
And earth were heaven's substitute,
    If thou were left to make it smile!

Oh, mark how soft the dipping oar,
    That silent cleaves the yielding blue—
Oh list, the low, sweet melody
    Of waves that beat our vessel too!

Oh, look to heaven, how pure it seems,
    No cloud to dim, no blot, no stain,
And say—if we refuse to love,
    Ought we to hope or smile again?

That island green, with roses gemmed,
    Let's seek it, love—how sweet a spot?
Then let the hours of night speed on,
    We live to love—it matters not!

The Stolen White Girl

The prairies are broad, and the woodlands are wide
And proud on his steed the wild half-breed may ride,
With the belt round his waist and the knife at his side.
And no white man may claim his beautiful bride.

Though he stole her away from the land of the whites,
Pursuit is in vain, for her bosom delights
In the love that she bears the dark-eyed, the proud,
Whose glance is like starlight beneath a night-cloud.

Far down in the depths of the forest they'll stray,
Where the shadows like night are lingering all day;
Where the flowers are springing up wild at their feet,
And the voices of birds in the branches are sweet.

Together they'll roam by the streamlets that run,
O'ershadowed at times then meeting the sun—
The streamlets that soften their varying tune,
As up the blue heavens calm wanders the moon!

The contrast between them is pleasing and rare;
Her sweet eye of blue, and her soft silken hair,
Her beautiful waist, and her bosom of white
That heaves to the touch with a sense of delight;

His form more majestic and darker his brow,
Where the sun has imparted its liveliest glow—
An eye that grows brighter with passion's true fire,
As he looks on his loved one with earnest desire.

Oh, never let Sorrow's cloud darken their fate,
The girl of the "pale face," her Indian mate!
But deep in the forest of shadows and flowers,
Let Happiness smile, as she wings their sweet hours.

BRET HARTE (1836–1902) ✳ *Harte moved from the northeast to California when he was fifteen. He worked as a miner, stagecoach guard, teacher, express messenger, printer, and literary journalist. He became the first editor of* The Overland Monthly, *established in 1868 in San Francisco to rival the* Atlantic *in Boston. In the second issue his story "The Luck of Roaring Camp" appeared, bringing him national fame. Harte was, thereafter, eagerly sought out by eastern editors and publishers. In 1871 he returned east to live in Boston, later moving to Europe as U.S. consul in Germany.*[11]

Plain Language from Truthful James

Table Mountain, 1870

Which I wish to remark,
    And my language is plain,
That for ways that are dark
    And for tricks that are vain,
The heathen Chinee is peculiar,
    Which the same I would rise to explain.

Ah Sin was his name;
    And I shall not deny,
In regard to the same,
    What that name might imply;
But his smile it was pensive and childlike,
    As I frequent remarked to Bill Nye.

It was August the third,
    And quite soft was the skies;
Which it might be inferred
    That Ah Sin was likewise;
Yet he played it that day upon William
    And me in a way I despise.

Which we had a small game,
 And Ah Sin took a hand:
It was Euchre. The same
 He did not understand;
But he smiled as he sat by the table,
 With the smile that was childlike and bland.

Yet the cards they were stocked
 In a way that I grieve,
And my feelings were shocked
 At the state of Nye's sleeve,
Which was stuffed full of aces and bowers,
 And the same with intent to deceive.

But the hands that were played
 By that heathen Chinee,
And the points that he made,—
 Were quite frightful to see,—
Till at last he put down a right bower,
 Which the same Nye had dealt unto me.

Then I looked up at Nye,
 And he gazed upon me;
And he rose with a sigh,
 And said, "Can this be?
We are ruined by Chinese cheap labor,"—
 And he went for that heathen Chinee.

Poker party at John Doyle's ranch, Arizona, 1887—1889. PHOTO: A.E. AMES.

In the scene that ensued
    I did not take a hand,
But the floor it was strewed
    Like the leaves on the strand
With the cards that Ah Sin had been hiding,
    In the game "he did not understand."

In his sleeves, which were long,
    He had twenty-four jacks,—
Which was coming it strong,
    Yet I state but the facts;
And we found on his nails, which were taper,
    What is frequent in tapers,—that's wax.

Which is why I remark,
    And my language is plain,
That for ways that are dark
    And for tricks that are vain,
The heathen Chinee is peculiar,—
    Which the same I am free to maintain.

The Society Upon the Stanislaus

I reside at Table Mountain, and my name is Truthful James;
I am not up to small deceit or any sinful games;
And I'll tell in simple language what I know about the row
That broke up our Society upon the Stanislow.

But first I would remark, that it is not a proper plan
For any scientific gent to whale his fellow-man,
And, if a member don't agree with his peculiar whim,
To lay for that same member for to "put a head" on him.

Now nothing could be finer or more beautiful to see
Than the first six months' proceedings of that same Society,
Till Brown of Calaveras brought a lot of fossil bones
That he found within a tunnel near the tenement of Jones.

Then Brown he read a paper, and he reconstructed there,
From those same bones, an animal that was extremely rare;
And Jones then asked the Chair for a suspension of the rules,
Till he could prove that those same bones was one of his lost mules.

Then Brown he smiled a bitter smile, and said he was at fault,
It seemed he had been trespassing on Jones's family vault;
He was a most sarcastic man, this quiet Mr. Brown,
And on several occasions he had cleaned out the town.

Now I hold it is not decent for a scientific gent
To say another is an ass,—at least, to all intent;
Nor should the individual who happens to be meant
Reply by heaving rocks at him, to any great extent.

Then Abner Dean of Angel's raised a point of order, when
A chunk of old red sandstone took him in the abdomen,
And he smiled a kind of sickly smile, and curled up on the floor,
And the subsequent proceedings interested him no more.

For, in less time than I write it, every member did engage
In a warfare with the remnants of the paleozoic age;
And the way they heaved those fossils in their anger was a sin,
Till the skull of an old mammoth caved the head of Thompson in.

And this is all I have to say of these improper games,
For I live at Table Mountain, and my name is Truthful James;
And I've told in simple language what I know about the row
That broke up our Society upon the Stanislow.

JOAQUIN MILLER (1837–1913) ✳

Pilgrims of the Plains

A tale half told and hardly understood;
The talk of bearded men that chanced to meet,
That lean'd on long quaint rifles in the wood,
That look'd in fellow faces, spoke discreet
And low, as half in doubt and in defeat
Of hope; a tale it was of lands of gold
That lay below the sun. Wild-wing'd and fleet
It spread among the swift Missouri's bold
Unbridled men, and reach'd to where Ohio roll'd.

Cincinnatus Hiner Miller was born in Indiana, the son of a Quaker schoolteacher. In 1852 he crossed the plains with his family, settling in the Willamette Valley in Oregon. He left home at age fifteen to mine gold in northern California and lived there with Modoc Indians. He later taught school, practiced law, rode the pony express through Oregon, Washington, and Idaho, became a newspaper editor, and planted orchards. He became known as "the Bard of the Sierras," and "the Byron of Oregon." He took his name from the Mexican bandit Joaquin Murietta, and attracted renown in the United States and in Europe with his flamboyant western style, which frequently featured sombrero, buckskins, and spurs.[12]

Covered wagon and pioneer family, Loup Valley, Nebraska, 1886.

Then long chain'd lines of yoked and patient steers;
Then long white trains that pointed to the west,
Beyond the savage west; the hopes and fears
Of blunt, untutor'd men, who hardly guess'd
Their course; the brave and silent women, dress'd
In homely spun attire, the boys in bands,
The cheery babes that laugh'd at all, and bless'd
The doubting hearts, with laughing lifted hands! . . .
What exodus for far untraversed lands!

The Plains! The shouting drivers at the wheel;
The crash of leather whips; the crush and roll
Of wheels; the groan of yokes and grinding steel
And iron chain, and lo! at last the whole
Vast line, that reach'd as if to touch the goal,
Began to stretch and stream away and wind
Toward the west, as if with one control;
Then hope loom'd fair, and home lay far behind;
Before, the boundless plain, and fiercest of their kind.

At first the way lay green and fresh as seas
And far away as any reach of wave;
The sunny streams went by in belt of trees;
And here and there the tassell'd tawny brave
Swept by on horse, look'd back, stretch'd forth and gave
A yell of hell, and then did wheel and rein
Awhile, and point away, dark brow'd and grave,
Into the far and dim and distant plain
With signs and prophecies, and then plunged on again.

Some hills at last began to lift and break;
Some streams began to fail of wood and tide,
The somber plain began betime to take
A hue of weary brown, and wild and wide
It stretch'd its naked breast on every side.
A babe was heard at last to cry for bread
Amid the deserts; cattle low'd and died,
And dying men went by with broken tread,
And left a long black serpent line of wreck and dead.

Strange hunger'd birds, black-wing'd and still as death,
And crown'd of red with hooked beaks, flew low
And close about, till we could touch their breath—
Strange unnamed birds, that seem'd to come and go
In circles now, and now direct and slow,
Continual, yet never touch the earth;
Slim foxes slid and shuttled to and fro
At times across the dusty weary dearth
Of life, look'd back, then sank like crickets in a hearth.

Then dust arose, a long dim line like smoke
From out of riven earth. The wheels went groaning by,
The thousand feet in harness and in yoke,
They tore the ways of ashen alkali,
And desert winds blew sudden, swift and dry.
The dust! it sat upon and fill'd the train!
It seem'd to fret and fill the very sky.
Lo! dust upon the beasts, the tent, the plain,
And dust, alas! on breasts that rose not up again.

They sat in desolation and in dust
By dried-up desert streams; the mother's hands
Hid all her bended face; the cattle thrust
Their tongues and faintly call'd across the lands.
The babes, that knew not what the way through sands
Could mean, did ask if it would end today . . .
The panting wolves slid by, red-eyed, in bands
To pools beyond. The men look'd far away,
And silent deemed that all a boundless desert lay.

They rose by night; they struggled on and on
As thin and still as ghosts; then here and there
Beside the dusty way before the dawn,
Men silent laid them down in their despair,
And died. But woman! Woman, frail as fair!
May man have strength to give to you your due;
You falter'd not, nor murmur'd anywhere,
You held your babes, held to your course, and you
Bore on through burning hell your double burdens through.

Men stood at last, the decimated few,
Above a land of running streams, and they?
They push'd aside the boughs, and peering through
Beheld afar the cool, refreshing bay;
Then some did curse, and some bend hands to pray;
But some look'd back upon the desert, wide
And desolate with death, then all the day
They mourned. But one, with nothing left beside
His dog to love, crept down among the ferns and died.

INA COOLBRITH (1841–1928) ✳

Born Josephine Donna Smith, niece of poet Eliza R. Snow, Ina Coolbrith came west by the Overland Trail at age ten, a member of the first party through Beckwourth Pass to California. Her family settled in Los Angeles, then a little town of Mexican pueblos, where she wrote and published her first poems. After an early and tumultuous marriage, she divorced, moved to San Francisco, and took her mother's maiden name. There she became associated with Bret Harte and Charles Warren Stoddard— the three became known as the "Golden Gate Trinity"—and hosted a weekly salon that entertained Joaquin Miller, John Muir, Isadora Duncan, and many others. She published three volumes of poetry and was appointed California's poet laureate in 1915, the first female laureate in the United States.[13]

Longing

O foolish wisdom sought in books!
   O aimless fret of household tasks!
O chains that bind the hand and mind—
   A fuller life my spirit asks!

For there the grand hills, summer-crowned,
   Slope greenly downward to the seas;
One hour of rest upon their breast
   Were worth a year of days like these.

Their cool, soft green to ease the pain
   Of eyes that ache o'er printed words;
This weary noise—the city's voice,
   Lulled in the sound of bees and birds.

For Eden's life within me stirs,
   And scorns the shackles that I wear;
The man-life grand—pure soul, strong hand,
   The limb of steel, the heart of air!

And I could kiss, with longing wild,
   Earth's dear brown bosom, loved so much,
A grass-blade fanned across my hand,
   Would thrill me like a lover's touch.

The trees would talk with me; the flowers
　　Their hidden meanings each make known—
The olden lore revived once more,
　　When man's and nature's heart were one!

And as the pardoned pair might come
　　Back to the garden God first framed,
And hear Him call at even-fall,
　　And answer, "Here am I," unshamed—

So I, from out these toils, wherein
　　The Eden-faith grows stained and dim,
Would walk, a child, through nature's wild,
　　And hear His voice and answer Him.

The Captive of the White City[*]

Flower of the foam of the waves
　　Of the beautiful inland sea,—
White as the foam that laves
　　The ships of the Sea-Kings past,—
　　　　Marvel of human hands,
Wonderful, mystical, vast,
　　　　The great White City stands;
And the banners of all the lands
Are free on the western breeze,
　　　　Free as the West is free.

*"The White City" was the name given to the Columbian Exposition in Chicago, 1893. The man who killed General Custer on the Little Bighorn was displayed in the Midway Plaisance of the fair. He sat, under guard, in a log cabin brought from Montana and reportedly owned by Sitting Bull, the same cabin in which that chief and his son had been killed.

And the throngs go up and down
In the streets of the wonderful town
    In brotherly love and grace,—
Children of every zone
The light of the sun has known:
      And there in the Midway Place,
    In the House of the Unhewn Trees,
There in the surging crowd,
Silent, and stern, and proud,
      Sits Rain-in-the-Face!

Why is the captive here?
Is the hour of the Lord so near
When slayer and slain shall meet
In the place of the Judgment seat
    For the word of the last decree?
    Ah, what is that word to be?
For the beautiful City stands
On the Red Man's wrested lands,[*]
      The home of a fated race;
And a ghostly shadow falls
Over the trophied walls[**]
    Of the House of the Unhewn Tree,
      In the pleasant Midway Place.
There is blood on the broken door,
There is blood on the broken floor,
Blood on your bronzed hands,
    O Rain-in-the-Face.

[*]The Indians claim that the land upon which
Chicago is built was never fully paid for.

[**]"The walls were hung with relics of the fight"
[Coolbrith's note].

"Our first grizzly": killed by General Custer and Colonel Ludlow during Black Hills expedition.

PHOTO: ILLINGWORTH.

Shut from the sunlit air,
Like a sun-god overthrown,
    The soldier, Custer, lies.
Dust is the sun-kissed hair,
    Dust are the dauntless eyes,
Dust and a name alone;—
    While the wife holds watch with grief
    For the never-returning chief.
What if she walked to-day
In the City's pleasant way,
    The beautiful Midway Place,
    And there to her sudden gaze,
Dimmed with her widow's tears,
    After the terrible years,
    Stood Rain-in-the-Face!

Quench with a drop of dew
From the morning's cloudless blue
    The prairies' burning plains—
    The seas of seething flame;
Turn from its awful path
The tempest, in its wrath;
    Lure from his jungle-lair
    The tiger, crouching there
For the leap on his sighted prey:
    Then seek as well to tame
The hate in the Red Man's veins,
His tiger-thirst to cool,
    In the hour of the evil day
When his foe before him stands!

From the wrongs of the White Man's rule
Blood only may wash the trace.
Alas, for the death-heaped slain!
Alas for your blood-stained hands,
    O Rain-in-the-Face!

And the throngs go up, go down,
In the streets of the wonderful town;
And jests of the merry tongue,
And the dance, and the glad songs sung,
    Ring through the sunlit space.
And there, in the wild, free breeze,
In the House of the Unhewn Trees,
    In the beautiful Midway Place,
        The captive sits apart,
        Silent, and makes no sign.
        But what is the word in your heart,
    O man of a dying race?
What tale on your lips for mine,
    O Rain-in-the-Face?

American Indian Songs
(Late nineteenth to mid-twentieth century) ✳

The work of anthropologists, ethnologists, linguists, and other researchers from the late nineteenth to the mid-twentieth century resulted in the gathering of a prodigious range of traditional Indian songs from hundreds of tribes. The act of transcribing the songs entailed not only the risks of inaccurate translation but the further diminishment of separating the words from their ritual purposes. What follows is a modest sampling from those materials, presented with the caution that these selections can convey only a shadow of the rich oral tradition of American Indian song, prayer, and storytelling.

Hopi[14]

Song of Creation

The dark purple light rises in the north,
A yellow light rises in the east.
Then we of the flowers of the earth come forth
To receive a long life of joy.
We call ourselves the Butterfly Maidens.

Both male and female make their prayers to the east,
Make the respectful sign to the Sun our Creator.
The sounds of bells ring through the air,
Making a joyful sound throughout the land,
Their joyful echo resounding everywhere.

Humbly I ask my Father,
The perfect one, Taiowa, our Father,
The perfect one creating the beautiful life
Shown to us by the yellow light,
To give us perfect light at the time of the red light.

The perfect one laid out the perfect plan
And gave to us a long span of life,
Creating song to implant joy in life.
On this path of happiness, we the Butterfly Maidens
Carry out his wishes by greeting our Father Sun.

The song resounds back from our Creator with joy.
And we of the earth repeat it to our Creator.
At the appearing of the yellow light,
Repeats and repeats again the joyful echo,
Sounds and resounds for times to come.

(Translated by Frank Waters)

Zuni[15]

Invocation to the U'wannami (Rain-Makers)

Come you, ascend the ladder; all come in; all sit down.
We were poor, poor, poor, poor, poor, poor,
When we came to this world through the poor place,
Where the body of water dried for our passing.
Banked up clouds cover the earth.
All come four times with your showers,
Descend to the base of the ladder and stand still;
Bring your showers and great rains.
All, all come, all ascend, all come in, all sit down.

✻

Masked "Mud Heads" prepare to dance, Zuni Pueblo, New Mexico, 1879. PHOTO: JOHN K. HILLERS.

Rain-makers, come out from all roads that great rivers may cover the earth;

That stones may be moved by the torrents;

That trees may be uprooted and moved by the torrents.

Great rain-makers, come out from all roads, carry the sands of our earth mother of the place.

Cover the earth with her heart, that all seeds may develop,

That my children may have all things to eat and be happy;

That the people of the outlying villages may all laugh and be happy;

That the growing children may all have things to eat and be happy.

This way our great father 'kǐa'ĕttonĕ wishes you to come.

This way our great mother chu'ĕttonĕ wishes you to come;

That we may have all kinds of seeds and all things good;

That we may inhale the sacred breath of life;

That our fathers 'kǐa'ĕttowe and our mothers chu'ĕttowe may bring us happy days.

Let our children live and be happy.

Send us the good south winds.

Send us your breath over the lakes that our great world may be made beautiful and our people may live.

✴

There, far off, my Sun Father arises, ascends the ladder, comes forth from his place.

May all complete the road of life, may all grow old.

May the children inhale more of the sacred breath of life.

May all my children have corn that they may complete the road of life.

Here sit down; here remain; we give you our best thoughts.

Hasten over the meal road; we are jealous of you.

We inhale the sacred breath through our prayer plumes.

(Translated by Matilda Coxe Stevenson)

Tewa[16]

Song of the Sky Loom

O our Mother the Earth, O our Father the Sky,
Your children are we, and with tired backs
We bring you the gifts you love.
Then weave for us a garment of brightness;
May the warp be the white light of morning.
May the weft be the red light of evening,
May the fringes be the falling rain,
May the border be the standing rainbow.
Thus weave for us a garment of brightness,
That we may walk fittingly where birds sing,
That we may walk fittingly where grass is green,
O our Mother the Earth, O our Father the Sky.

(Translated by Herbert J. Spinden)

Chiricahua Apache[17]

Song for Girls' Puberty Rites

I

I come to White Painted Woman,
By means of long life I come to her.
I come to her by means of her blessing,
I come to her by means of her good fortune,
I come to her by means of all different fruits.
By means of the long life she bestows, I come to her.
By means of this holy truth she goes about.

2
I am about to sing this song of yours,
The song of long life.
Sun, I stand here on the earth with your song,
Moon, I have come in with your song.

3
White Painted Woman's power emerges,
Her power for sleep.
White Painted Woman carries this girl;
She carries her through long life,
She carries her to good fortune,
She carries her to old age,
She bears her to peaceful sleep.

4
You have started out on the good earth;
You have started out with good moccasins;
With moccasin strings of the rainbow, you have started out.
With moccasin strings of the sun rays, you have started out.
In the midst of plenty you have started out.

(Translated by Morris Edward Opler)

Pima[18]

Datura Hunting Song

I ate the thornapple leaves
   And the leaves made me dizzy.
I drank the thornapple flowers
   And the drink made me stagger.

The hunter, Bow-remaining,
   He overtook and killed me,
Cut and threw my horns away.
   The hunter, Reed-remaining,
He overtook and killed me,
   Cut and threw my feet away.

Now the flies become crazy
   And they drop with flapping wings.
The drunken butterflies sit
   With opening and shutting wings.

(Translated by Frank Russell)

Teton Sioux[19]

Wolf Song

A wolf
I considered myself
But I have eaten nothing
And I can scarcely stand

A wolf
I considered myself
But the owls are hooting
And I fear the night.

(Translated by Frances Densmore)

Cheyenne [20]

The Death Song of White Antelope*

Nothing lives long
Except the earth and the mountains.

(Translated by George Bird Grinnell)

Kwakiutl [21]

Prayer to the Black Bear

When the black bear is dead,
when it has been shot by the hunter,
the man sits down on the ground
at the right-hand side of the bear.
Then the man says, praying to it,
"Thank you, friend, that you did not
make me walk about in vain.
Now you have come to take mercy on me
so that I obtain game, that I
may inherit your power of getting easily
with your hands the salmon
that you catch. Now I will press
my right hand against your left hand,"

*White Antelope, at the age of seventy-five, was one of
hundreds of Cheyenne and Arapaho Indians killed by the
Colorado Cavalry in the Sand Creek massacre of 1864.
Chief Black Kettle called out to White Antelope to join
him in retreat, but the old chief refused, stood with arms
folded, and sang this song until he was shot.

says the man as he takes hold of
the left paw of the bear. He says,
"O, friend, now we press together
our working hands that you may
give over to me your power
of getting easily with your hands,
friend," says he. Now it is done
after this, for now he only
skins the bear after this.

(Translated by Franz Boas, adapted by Alison Deming)

Prayer to the Sockeye Salmon

O, Swimmers, this is the dream
given by you, to be the way of my
late grandfathers when they first
caught you at your playground
in this river. Now you will be
in the same way, Swimmers.

I do not club you twice,
for I do not wish to club to death
your souls so that you may
go home to the place
where you come from, Supernatural Ones,
you, givers of heavy weight.

Thank you, Swimmers, you,
Supernatural Ones, that you have come
to try to save our lives,

mine and my husband's, that we
may not die of hunger, you
Long-Life-Maker, protect us
that nothing evil may befall us, you,
Rich-Woman-Maker; and also
this, that we may meet again next year,
good, great Supernatural Ones.

(Translated by Franz Boas, adapted by Alison Deming)

Healing Prayer to the Salmon-Berry Vines

Don't be startled, Supernatural One,
by my coming and sitting down
to make a request of you, Supernatural One.
I mean this, this is the reason why I come to you.
I come to you to pray you, please,
to let me take some of your blanket,
Sore-Healer, that it may heal the burn of my child,
that, please, may heal up his burn, Supernatural One.

O, Supernatural One, now I put you on to the sore of my child
that you may lick off this great sickness, that you,
please, make it heal, you, Supernatural One,
that, please, it may heal up, please, you,
Healing-Woman, you, Long-Life-Maker, please
take pity on me that my mind may be at rest,
you, Supernatural One.

(Translated by Franz Boas, adapted by Alison Deming)

Warsong of the Kwakiutl

I am the thunder of my tribe.
I am the seamonster of my tribe.
I am the earthquake of my tribe.
When I start to fly the thunder resounds through the world.
When I am maddened, the voice of the seabear resounds through the world.

(Translated by Franz Boas)

Tohono O'odham (Papago)[22]

War Songs

Gray owl medicine man,
Come with me!
Yonder find my enemy
And make him helpless!

✳

The wind keeps running with me.
With it, I run far yonder.
My enemy dizzily staggers forward.

✳

Here I come forth!
With the wind I come forth
And come hither.
This, my cigarette smoke,
I blow against the enemy.

✳

Gopher medicine man,
Gnaw the bow
Of this my enemy.

＊

Hoot owl medicine man,
Cut the arrow feathers
Of this my enemy.

＊

Very angry
To the flat land he came,
My enemy,
Exceedingly angry.

Very angry
To the mountains he came,
My enemy,
Exceedingly angry.

＊

Coyote, our comrade.
We meet the enemy!
Tomorrow, fight!

(Translated by Ruth Murray Underhill)

Tohono O'odham: Owl Woman[23][*]

Healing Songs

Brown Owls come here in the blue evening,
They are hooting about,
They are shaking their wings and hooting.

✳

How shall I begin my song
In the blue night that is settling?
I will sit here and begin my song.

✳

The owl feather is rolling in this direction and beginning to sing.
The people listen and come to hear the owl feather
Rolling in this direction and beginning to sing.

✳

Early in the evening they come hooting about,
Some have small voices and some have large voices,
Some have voices of medium strength, hooting about.

✳

I cannot make out what I see.
In the dark I enter.
I cannot make out what I see

---

[*]Owl Woman, whose Spanish name was Juana Maxwell, was a traditional Papago healer from San Xavier in Arizona. She was given her songs by spirits returned from the dead, and she used them in treatment of the sick. She reported that the dead stayed near their graves during the day, but at night they went to the spirit land by a road that was not far away. Only the spirits knew its location.

✳

Poor old sister, you have cared for this man and you want to see him again, but now his heart is almost covered with night. There is just a little left.

✳

Ahead of me some owl feathers are lying,
I hear something running toward me,
They pass by me, and farther ahead
I see spirit-tufts of downy white feathers.

✳

Yonder lies the spirit land.
Yonder the spirit land I see.
Farther ahead, in front of me,
I see a spirit stand.

✳

In the great night my heart will go out,
Toward me the darkness comes rattling,
In the great night my heart will go out.

(Translated by Frances Densmore)

Arapaho [24] *

Ghost Dance Songs

My children, when at first I liked the whites,
My children, when at first I liked the whites,
I gave them fruits,
I gave them fruits.

✳

Our father, the Whirlwind,
Our father, the Whirlwind,
Now wears the headdress of crow feathers,
Now wears the headdress of crow feathers.

✳

The Crow—Ehe'eye!
I saw him when he flew down,
To the earth, to the earth.
He has renewed our life.
He has taken pity on us.

✳

I hear everything,
I hear everything,
I am the crow,
I am the crow.

---

*During the 1890s the ghost dance movement swept through
the Plains tribes and on to the coastal and northwest Indians.
Many of the songs associated with these religious ceremonies
were wordless, made up of sounds, chanting, or sobbing. Many
described encounters with the dead or visions intelligible only
to the singer. Dances and rituals summoned the coming of a
Prophet, or a Whirlwind, that would bring in great change and
overthrow the whites.

✸

Our father is about to take pity on me,
Our father is about to take pity on me.
Our father is about to make me fly around.

✸

How bright is the moonlight!
How bright is the moonlight!
Tonight as I ride with my load of buffalo meat,
Tonight as I ride with my load of buffalo meat.

✸

I circle around—
I circle around
The boundaries of the earth
The boundaries of the earth—
Wearing the long wing feathers as I fly,
Wearing the long wing feathers as I fly.

✸

I'yehé my children
I'yehé my children
I'yehé we have rendered them desolate
I'yehé we have rendered them desolate
The whites are crazy.

✸

Father, have pity on me,
Father, have pity on me.
I am crying for thirst,
I am crying for thirst.
All is gone—I have nothing to eat.
All is gone—I have nothing to eat.

✳

My children, my children,
Look! the earth is about to move,
Look! the earth is about to move,
My father tells me so,
My father tells me so.

✳

My children—E'e'ye'!
My children—E'e'ye'!
Here it is, I hand it to you,
The earth—E'e'ye'!
The earth—E'e'ye'!

✳

Father, the Morning Star!
Father, the Morning Star!
Look on us, we have danced until daylight,
Look on us, we have danced until daylight.
Take pity on us—Hi'i'i'!
Take pity on us—Hi'i'i'!

(Translated by James Mooney)

Navajo[25][*]

from The Night Chant

In Tse'gihi,
In the house made of the dawn,
In the house made of the evening twilight,
In the house made of the dark cloud,
In the house made of the he-rain,
In the house made of the dark mist,
In the house made of the she-rain,
In the house made of pollen,
In the house made of grasshoppers,
Where the dark mist curtains the doorway,
The path to which is on the rainbow,
Where the zigzag lightning stands high on top,
Where the he-rain stands high on top,
Oh, male divinity!
With your moccasins of dark cloud, come to us.
With your leggings of dark cloud, come to us.
With your shirt of dark cloud, come to us.
With your headdress of dark cloud, come to us.
With your mind enveloped in dark cloud, come to us.
With the dark thunder above you, come to us soaring.
With the shapen cloud at your feet, come to us soaring.
With the far darkness made of the dark cloud over your head, come to us soaring.

[*]The Night Chant is a complex, integrated, nine-day healing ceremony that includes songs, dancing, ritual acts, and prayers. Washington Matthews, born in 1843, lived for eight years among the Navajo in New Mexico and Arizona. He first witnessed the ritual in 1880 and spent the next twenty-one years studying it. He reported that the ceremony's purpose is to repulse evil and attract holiness. One shaman told Matthews that he had studied for six years before he was competent to conduct the ceremony, and that he had learned much after that.

With the far darkness made of the he-rain over your head, come to us soaring.

With the far darkness made of the dark mist over your head, come to us soaring.

With the far darkness made of the she-rain over your head, come to us soaring.

With the zigzag lightning flung out on high over your head, come to us soaring.

With the rainbow hanging high over your head, come to us soaring.

With the far darkness made of the dark cloud on the ends of your wings, come to us soaring.

With the far darkness made of the he-rain on the ends of your wings, come to us soaring.

With the far darkness made of the dark mist on the ends of your wings, come to us soaring.

With the far darkness made of the she-rain on the ends of your wings, come to us soaring.

With the zigzag lightning flung out on high on the ends of your wings, come to us soaring.

With the rainbow hanging high on the ends of your wings, come to us soaring.

With the near darkness made of the dark cloud, of the he-rain, of the dark mist and of the she-rain, come to us.

With the darkness on the earth, come to us.

With these I wish the foam floating on the flowing water over the roots of the great corn.

I have made your sacrifice.

I have prepared a smoke for you.

My feet restore for me.

My limbs restore me.

My body restore me.

My mind restore me.

My voice restore me.

Today, take out your spell for me.

Today, take away your spell for me.

Away from me you have taken it.

Far off from me it is taken.

Far off you have done it.

Happily I recover.

Happily my interior becomes cool.

Happily my eyes regain their power.

Happily my head becomes cool.

Happily my limbs regain their power.

Happily I hear again.

Navajo Weaver, Torreon, New Mexico. PHOTO: MILTON SNOW.

Happily for me (the spell) is taken off.

Happily I walk (or, may I walk).

Impervious to pain, I walk.

Feeling light within, I walk.

With lively feelings, I walk.

Happily (or in beauty) abundant dark clouds I desire.

Happily abundant dark mists I desire.

Happily abundant passing showers I desire.

Happily an abundance of vegetation I desire.

Happily an abundance of pollen I desire.

Happily abundant dew I desire.

Happily may fair white corn, to the ends of the earth, come with you.

Happily may fair yellow corn, to the ends of the earth, come with you.

Happily may fair blue corn, to the ends of the earth, come with you.

Happily may fair corn of all kinds, to the ends of the earth, come with you.

Happily may fair plants of all kinds, to the ends of the earth, come with you.

Happily may fair goods of all kinds, to the ends of the earth, come with you.

Happily may fair jewels of all kinds, to the ends of the earth, come with you.

With these before you, happily may they come with you.

With these behind you, happily may they come with you.

With these below you, happily may they come with you.

With these above you, happily may they come with you.

With these all around you, happily may they come with you.

Thus happily you accomplish your tasks.

Happily the old men will regard you.

Happily the old women will regard you.

Happily the young men will regard you.

Happily the young women will regard you.

Happily the boys will regard you.

Happily the girls will regard you.

Happily the children will regard you.

Happily the chiefs will regard you.

Navajo papoose on a cradleboard, 1936.

PHOTO: H. ARMSTRONG ROBERTS.

Happily, as they scatter in different directions, they will regard you.

Happily, as they approach their homes, they will regard you.

Happily may their roads home be on the trail of pollen (peace).

Happily may they all get back.

In beauty (happily) I walk.

With beauty before me, I walk.

With beauty behind me, I walk.

With beauty below me, I walk.

With beauty above me, I walk.

With beauty all around me, I walk.

It is finished (again) in beauty.

It is finished in beauty.

It is finished in beauty.

It is finished in beauty.

(Translated by Washington Matthews)

EDWIN MARKHAM (1852–1940) ✳

Born in the Oregon Territory, Markham grew up on a ranch in northern California. He worked as a teacher, principal, and school superintendent at Placerville and was a student of spiritualism and socialism. Publication of "The Man with the Hoe" in the San Francisco Examiner *in January 1899 made him famous. He retired to Staten Island, New York, where his Sunday literary gatherings hosted Theodore Dreiser, Vachel Lindsay, and Edwin Arlington Robinson, among others. He founded the Poetry Society of America in 1910. Markham's eightieth birthday was celebrated with a reading and ceremony at Carnegie Hall; thirty-five nations sent representatives.*[26]

The Man with the Hoe

Written after seeing Millet's world-famous painting

> *God made man in His own image,*
> *in the image of God made He him.*
> *—Genesis*

Bowed by the weight of centuries he leans
Upon his hoe and gazes on the ground,
The emptiness of ages in his face,
And on his back the burden of the world.
Who made him dead to rapture and despair,
A thing that grieves not and that never hopes,
Stolid and stunned, a brother to the ox?
Who loosened and let down this brutal jaw?
Whose was the hand that slanted back this brow?
Whose breath blew out the light within this brain?

Is this the Thing the Lord God made and gave
To have dominion over sea and land;
To trace the stars and search the heavens for power;
To feel the passion of Eternity?
Is this the Dream he dreamed who shaped the suns
And pillared the blue firmament with light?

Down all the stretch of Hell to its last gulf
There is no shape more terrible than this—
More tongued with censure of the world's blind greed—
More filled with signs and portents for the soul—
More fraught with menace to the universe.

What gulfs between him and the seraphim!
Slave of the wheel of labor, what to him
Are Plato and the swing of Pleiades?
What the long reaches of the peaks of song,
The rift of dawn, the reddening of the rose?
Through this dread shape the suffering ages look;
Time's tragedy is in that aching stoop;
Through this dread shape humanity betrayed,
Plundered, profaned and disinherited,
Cries protest to the Judges of the World,
A protest that is also prophecy.

O masters, lords and rulers in all lands,
Is this the handiwork you give to God,
This monstrous thing distorted and soul-quenched?
How will you ever straighten up this shape;
Touch it again with immortality;
Give back the upward looking and the light;
Rebuild in it the music and the dream;
Make right the immemorial infamies,
Perfidious wrongs, immedicable woes?

O masters, lords and rulers in all lands,
How will the Future reckon with this Man?
How answer his brute question in that hour
When whirlwinds of rebellion shake the world?
How will it be with kingdoms and with kings—
With those who shaped him to the thing he is—
When the dumb Terror shall reply to God,
After the silence of the centuries?

In Death Valley

There came gray stretches of volcanic plains,
Bare, lone and treeless, then a bleak lone hill,
Like to the dolorous hill that Dobell saw.
Around were heaps of ruins piled between
The Burn o' Sorrow and the Water o' Care;
And from the stillness of the down-crushed walls
One pillar rose up dark against the moon.
There was a nameless Presence everywhere;
In the gray soil there was a purple stain,
And the gray reticent rocks were dyed with blood—
Blood of a vast unknown Calamity.
It was the mark of some ancestral grief—
Grief that began before the ancient Flood.

Death valley. PHOTO: ANSEL ADAMS.

MARY AUSTIN (1868–1934) ✳

*Austin, a novelist, playwright, and folklorist, won critical acclaim for her prose works—*A Woman of Genius, The Land of Little Rain, *and* The Flock—*and for her plays, poems, and essays about Indians of the Southwest. Born in the Midwest, she lived for more than twenty years in California, where she was associated with the Carmel literary community. Moving in 1918 to Santa Fe, Austin explored her interests in Spanish-American culture and American Indian poetics. Her theory of poetics, published in* The American Rhythm *in 1923, proposed that rhythms in poetry derive from the land, that "verse forms are shaped by topography and the rhythm of food supply." She claimed that by listening to recordings of unidentified American Indian songs, she could tell from the rhythms if the verse came from a desert, plains, or woodland tribe.*[27]

The Grass on the Mountain

Oh, long, long
The snow has possessed the mountains.

The deer have come down and the big-horn,
They have followed the Sun to the south
To feed on the mesquite pods and the bunch grass.
Loud are the thunder drums
In the tents of the mountains.

Oh, long, long
Have we eaten *chia* seeds
And dried deer's flesh of the summer killing.
We are wearied of our huts
And the smoky smell of our garments.

We are sick with desire of the sun
And the grass on the mountain.

(from the Paiute)

Song of a Man About to Die in a Strange Land[*]

If I die here
In a strange land,
If I die
In a land I do not know,
Nevertheless, the thunder,
The rolling thunder will take me home.

If I die here, the wind,
The wind rushing over the prairie,
The wind will take me home.

The wind and the thunder
They are the same everywhere.
What does it matter then,
If I die in a strange land.

Song of the Maverick

I am too arid for tears, and for laughter
Too sore with unslaked desires.
My nights are scanty of sleep
And my sleep too full of dreaming;
The frosts are not cold enough
Nor the suns sufficiently burning:
The hollow waves are slack
And no wind from any quarter

[*]This is a Chippewa Song, which was sung to encourage a good spirit in the young. The
Chippewas are the same as the Ojibways, and once lived about the Great Lakes.
They are now much scattered, some of them being in Kansas and the Southwest. [Austin's note]

Lifts strongly enough to outwear me.
My body is bitter with baffled lusts
Of work and love and endurance.
As a maverick, leaderless, lost from the herd,
Loweth my soul with the need of man encounters.

For I am crammed and replete
With the power of desolate places;
I have gone far on faint trails
And slept in the shade of my arrows;
Patience, forgiveness and might
Ache in me, finding no egress,
And virtues stale that are too big for the out gate.

I would run large with the man herd, the hill subduers,
I would impress myself on the mold of large adventure
Until all deeds of that likeness
Should a long time carry
The stripe of the firstling's father.

For I am anguished with strength,
Overfed with the common experience,
My feet run wide of the rutted trails
Toward the undared destinies.

FRANK BIRD LINDERMAN (1869–1938) ✳

Linderman came west from Ohio when he was sixteen years old, having dreamed of doing so since he was a child. He settled on Flathead Lake in western Montana and lived as trapper, guide, newspaperman, businessman, and politician. Between 1915 and 1935 he published fifteen books—Indian legends, nonfiction, novels, and one book of poems. His most significant achievements were two books, both based on firsthand interviews, about American Indian experience: American: The Life Story of a Great Indian, Plenty-Coups, Chief of the Crows *and* Red Mother, *reminiscences of the old medicine woman Pretty Shield.*[28]

Cabins

They was dirt-roofed, an' homely, an' ramblin', an' squat—
Jest logs with mud-daubin'; but I loved 'em a lot.
Their latch-strings was out, an' their doors wouldn't lock:
Get down an' walk in ('twas politer to knock).
Mebby nobody home, but the grub was still there;
He'p yerse'f, leave a note, to show you was square;
Might be gone for a week; stay as long as you please,
You knowed you was welcome as a cool summer breeze;
Might be spring 'fore you'd see him, then he'd grin an' declare
He'd a-give a good hoss if he'd only been there.
But he's gone with his smile, an' the dear little shack
With his brand on its door won't never come back.
An' his latch-string is hid with the spirit an' ways
That gladdened our hearts in them good early days.
There wasn't a fence in the world that we knew,
For the West an' its people was honest an' new,
And the range spread away with the sky for a lid—
I'm old, but I'm glad that I lived when I did.

Trappers and hunters in front of cabin in the Four Peaks country in Brown's basin, 1908.   PHOTO: LUBKIN.

In 1882 Hall moved with her family from Kansas to Arizona. She managed two ranches, hers and her parents', wrote for and edited Charles F. Lummis's magazine Out West, *served as Arizona's Territorial Historian (the first woman in the territory to hold public office), and undertook various research expeditions. In her preface to the second edition of* Cactus and Pine, *from which collection these poems are taken, she reported that the plates of the first edition, published in Boston, had been melted down in a World War I munitions factory and were "shot at the Hun," thereby doing "their part in winning the war in a decidedly original way for poetry."*[29]

Poppies of Wickenburg

The great fields of yellow poppies that blossom around Wickenburg in the very early spring were first described by the veteran botanist and traveller of the Fifties, John Cowan. They have been the delight of many travellers since that time.

Where Coronado's men of old
Sought the Pecos' fabled gold
Vainly many weary days,
Now the land is all ablaze.

Where the desert breezes stir,
Earth, the old sun-worshipper,
Lifts her shining chalices
Up to tempt the priestly bees.

Every golden cup is filled
With a nectar sun-distilled;
And the perfumes, Nature's prayer,
Sweetens all the desert air.

Poppies, poppies, who would stray
O'er the mountains far away,
Seeking Quivira's gold,
When your wealth is ours to hold?

Boot Hill

In the days of the Old Frontier the graveyard in every mining camp and
cow town was called "Boot Hill"—because many of its inmates died
literally "with their boots on." Today these forgotten graveyards, with their
sunken, half-obliterated graves, are all that is left of many a once-thriving
"Burg." Their nameless dead are the drift that marks forgotten channels
where once the tide of human life flowed full and strong.

Go softly, you whose careless feet
Would crush the sage brush, pungent, sweet,
And brush the rabbit weed aside
From burrows where the ground squirrels hide,
And prairie dog his watch-tower keeps
Among the ragged gravel heaps.
Year long the wind blows up and down
Each lessening mound, and drifts the brown
Dried "wander-weed" there at their feet—
Who no more wander, slow or fleet.
Sun-bleached, rain-warped, the head-boards hold
One story, all too quickly told:
That here some wild heart takes its rest
From spent desire and fruitless quest.

Here in the grease-wood's scanty shade
How many a daring soul was laid!
Boots on—full-garbed as when he died—
The pistol belted at his side;
The worn sombrero on his breast—
To prove another man the best.
Arrow or knife, or quick-drawn gun—
The glad, mad, fearless game was done.
A life for stakes—play slow or fast—
Win—lose—yet Death held trumps at last.

Some went where bar room tinsel flared,
Or painted dance hall wantons stared;—
Some, where the lone, brown ranges bared
Their parched length to a parching sky;
And God, alone, might hear the cry
Of thirst-dried lips that, stiff and cold,
Seemed still to babble: "Gold, gold, gold!"
Woman or wine or greed or Chance;—
A comrade's shot—an Indian lance;
By camp or cañon, trail or street—
Here all games end—here all trails meet.

The ground squirrels chatter in the sun;
The dry, gray sage leaves, one by one,
Drift down, close-curled, in odorous heaps.
Above, wide-winged, a wild hawk sweeps;
And on the worn board at the head
Of one whose name was fear and dread,
A little, solemn ground owl sits.
Ah, here the Man and Life are Quits!
Go softly, nor with careless feet—
Here all games end—here all trails meet.

WILLA CATHER (1876–1947) ✳ *Born in Virginia, Cather was nine when her family moved to the Nebraska prairie frontier. In 1904, after graduating from the University of Nebraska, she moved to New York City; the next year her first book of stories was published, leading to her editorial position at* McClure's Magazine. *She is considered one of the great writers of the century; her most enduring fiction explores the lives of frontier settlers on the prairies and in colonial New Mexico. She published one volume of poetry.*[30]

Spanish Johnny

The old West, the old time,
   The old wind singing through
The red, red grass a thousand miles.
   And, Spanish Johnny, you!
He'd sit beside the water-ditch
   When all his herd was in,
And never mind a child, but sing
   To his mandolin.

The big stars, the blue night,
   The moon-enchanted plain:
The olive man who never spoke,
   But sang the songs of Spain.
His speech with men was wicked talk—
   To hear it was a sin;
But those were golden things he said
   To his mandolin.

The gold songs, the gold stars,
   The world so golden then:
And the hand so tender to a child

Had killed so many men.
He died a hard death long ago
    Before the Road came in;
The night before he swung, he sang
    To his mandolin.

Prairie Spring

Evening and the flat land,
Rich and somber and always silent;
The miles of fresh-plowed soil,
Heavy and black, full of strength and harshness;
The growing wheat, the growing weeds,
The toiling horses, the tired men;
The long, empty roads,
Sullen fires of sunset, fading,
The eternal, unresponsive sky.
Against all this, Youth,
Flaming like the wild roses,
Singing like the larks over the plowed fields,
Flashing like a star out of the twilight;
Youth with its unsupportable sweetness,
Its fierce necessity,
Its sharp desire;
Singing and singing,
Out of the lips of silence
Out of the earthy dusk.

Initiating one of the new
arrivals at the planting camp,
Nebraska Forest, 1914.

Macon Prairie

(Nebraska)

She held me for a night against her bosom,
The aunt who died when I was yet a baby,
The girl who scarcely lived to be a woman.
Stricken, she left familiar earth behind her,
Mortally ill, she braved the boisterous ocean,
Dying, she crossed irrevocable rivers,
Hailed the blue Lakes, and saw them fade forever,
Hungry for distances;—her heart exulting
That God had made so many seas and countries
To break upon the eye and sweep behind her.
From one whose love was tempered by discretion,
From all the net of caution and convenience
She snatched her high heart for the great adventure,
Broke her bright bubble under far horizons,—
Among the skirmishers that teased the future,
Precursors of the grave slow-moving millions
Already destined to the Westward-faring.

They came, at last, to where the railway ended,
The strange troop captained by a dying woman;
The father, the old man of perfect silence,
The mother, unresisting, broken-hearted,
The gentle brother and his wife, both timid,
Not knowing why they left their native hamlet;
Going as in a dream, but ever going.

In all the glory of an Indian summer,
The lambent transmutations of October,
They started with the great ox-teams from Hastings

And trekked in a southwesterly direction,
Boring directly toward the fiery sunset.
Over the red grass prairies, shaggy-coated,
Without a goal the caravan proceeded;
Across the tablelands and rugged ridges,
Through the coarse grasses which the oxen breasted,
Blue-stem and bunch-grass, red as sea-marsh samphire.
Always the similar, soft undulations
Of the free-breathing earth in golden sunshine,
The hardy wind, and dun hawks flying over
Against the unstained firmament of heaven.

In the front wagon, under the white cover,
Stretched on her feather-bed and propped with pillows,
Never dismayed by the rude oxen's scrambling,
The jolt of the tied wheel or brake or hold-back,
She lay, the leader of the expedition;
And with her burning eyes she took possession
Of the red waste,—for hers, and theirs, forever.

A wagon-top, rocking in seas of grasses,
A camp-fire on a prairie chartless, trackless,
A red spark under the dark tent of heaven.
Surely, they said, by day she saw a vision,
Though her exhausted strength could not impart it,—
Her breathing hoarser than the tired cattle.

When cold, bright stars the sunburnt days succeeded,
She took me in her bed to sleep beside her,—
A sturdy bunch of life, born on the ocean.
Always she had the wagon cover lifted
Before her face. The sleepless hours till daybreak
She read the stars.

"Plenty of time for sleep," she said, "hereafter."

She pointed out the spot on Macon prairie,
Telling my father that she wished to lie there.
"And plant, one day, an apple orchard round me,
In memory of woman's first temptation,
And man's first cowardice."
That night, within her bosom,
I slept.
                         Before the morning
I cried because the breast was cold behind me.

Now, when the sky blazes like blue enamel,
Brilliant and hard over the blond cornfields,
And through the autumn days our wind is blowing
Like the creative breath of God Almighty—
Then I rejoice that offended love demanded
Such wide retreat, and such self-restitution;
Forged an explorer's will in a frail woman,
Asked of her perfect faith and renunciation,
Hardships and perils, prophecy and vision,
The leadership of kin, and happy ending
On the red rolling land of Macon prairie.

WITTER BYNNER (1881–1968) ✳ *Bynner was a highly regarded poet early in the century, though his work is little known today. He lived for forty-six years in Santa Fe and traveled with D. H. and Frieda Lawrence on their first trip to Mexico. Among his best poems are those inspired by Indian life in the Southwest.*[31]

Snake Dance

(Hotevilla)

We are clean for them now, as naked-clean as they are,
We go out for them now and we meet them with our hands.
Bullsnakes, rattlesnakes, whipsnakes, we compare
Our cleanness with their cleanness. The sun stands
Witness, the moon stands witness. The dawn joins
Their scales with our flesh, the evening quiets their rattles.
We can feel their tails soothing along our loins
Like the feathers on our fathers after battles.
For their fathers were our fathers. We are brothers
Born of the earth and brothers in the sun;
And our destiny is only one another's,
However apart the races we have run.
Out of the earth we came, the sons of kings;
For the daughters of serpent-kings had offered grace
To our fathers and had formed us under their wings
To be worthy of light at last, body and face.
Out of the earth we came, into this open
Largeness of light, into this world we see
Lifted and laid along, broken and slopen,
This world that heaves toward heaven eternally.
We have found them, we have brought them, and we know them

As kin of us, because our fathers said:
As we have always shown them, you must show them
That kinship in the world is never dead.
Come then, O bullsnake, wake from your slow search
Across the desert. Here are your very kin.
Dart not away from us, whipsnake, but perch
Your head among your people moulded in
A greater shape yet touching the earth like you.
Leave off your rattling, rattlesnake, leave off
Your coiling, your venom. There is only dew
Under the starlight. Let our people cough
In the blowing sand and hide their faces, oh still
Receive them, know them, live with them in peace.
They want no rocks from you, none of your hill.
Uncoil again, lie on our arms, and cease
From the wars our fathers ceased from, be again
Close to your cousins, listen to our song.
Dance with us, kinsfolk, be with us as men
Descended from common ancestors, belong
To none but those who join yourselves and us.
Oh listen to the feathers that can weave
Only enchantment and to the words we sing,
The feet we touch the earth with. Help us believe
That our ancestors are still remembering.
Go back to them with sacred meal, go back
Down through the earth, oh be our messengers!
Tell them with reverence, tell them our lack;
Tell them we have no roots, but a sap that stirs
Forever unrooted upward to the sky.
But tell them also, tell them of our song
Downward from heaven, back where we belong.
Oh north, east, west and south, tell them we die!

JOHN G. NEIHARDT (1881–1973) ✳

Born on a farm in Illinois, Neihardt and his two sisters came west with their mother to live with her parents in a sod hut on the prairie. From 1901 to 1907 he lived among the Omaha Indians, who named him "Little Bull Buffalo," and later was poet-in-residence at the University of Missouri at Columbia. He began his great epic poem, A Cycle of the West, in 1912 and saw it published in 1949. The work contains five "Songs" that tell of heroic endeavors in the settlement of the West, beginning with the ascent of the upper Missouri River in 1822 and ending with the Battle of Wounded Knee in 1890—"a time," in Neihardt's words, "when an old culture was being overcome by that of a powerful people driven by the ancient needs and greeds." Neihardt's most lasting prose work is Black Elk Speaks, based on his recorded conversations with an Oglala Sioux holy man.[32]

from The Song of the Indian Wars

III. THE COUNCIL ON THE POWDER

          . . . Then Sitting Bull arose;
And through the stirring crowd a murmur 'woke
As of a river yielding to the stroke
Of some deft swimmer. No heroic height
Proclaimed him peer among the men of might,
Nor was his bearing such as makes men serve.
Bull-torsed, squat-necked, with legs that kept a curve
To fit the many ponies he had backed,
He scarcely pleased the eyes. But what he lacked
Of visible authority to mould
Men's lives, was compensated manifold
By something penetrating in his gaze
That searched the rabble, seeming to appraise
The common weakness that should make him strong.
One certainty about him held the throng—
His hatred of the white men. Otherwise,
Conjecture, interweaving truth and lies,
Wrought various opinions of the man.
A mountebank—so one opinion ran—
A battle-shirking intimate of squaws,
A trivial contriver of applause,

A user of the sacred for the base.
Yet there was something other in his face
Than vanity and craft. And there were those
Who saw him in that battle with the Crows
The day he did a thing no coward could.
There ran a slough amid a clump of wood
From whence, at little intervals, there broke
A roaring and a spurt of rifle-smoke
That left another wound among the Sioux.
Now Sitting Bull rode down upon the slough
To see what might be seen there. What he saw
Was such as might have gladdened any squaw—
A wounded warrior with an empty gun!
'Twas then that deed of Sitting Bull was done,
And many saw it plainly from the hill.
Would any coward shun an easy kill
And lose a scalp? Yet many saw him throw
His loaded rifle over to the Crow,
Retreat a space, then wheel to charge anew.
With but a riding quirt he counted *coup*
And carried back a bullet in his thigh.
Let those who jeered the story for a lie
Behold him limping yet! And others said
He had the gift of talking with the dead
And used their clearer seeing to foretell
Dark things aright; that he could weave a spell
To make a foeman feeble if he would.

Such things the people pondered while he stood
And searched them with a quiet, broad-browed stare.
Then suddenly some magic happened there.
Can men grow taller in a breathing span?

He spoke; and even scorners of the man
Were conscious of a swift, disarming thrill,
The impact of a dominating will
That overcame them.

               "Brothers, you have seen
The way the spring sun makes the prairie green
And wakes new life in animal and seed,
Preparing plenty for the biggest need,
Remembering the little hungers too.
The same mysterious quickening makes new
Men's hearts, for by that power we also live.
And so, till now, we thought it good to give
All life its share of what that power sends
To man and beast alike. But hear me, friends!
We face a greedy people, weak and small
When first our fathers met them, now grown tall
And overbearing. Tireless in toil,
These madmen think it good to till the soil,
And love for endless getting marks them fools.
Behold, they bind their poor with many rules
And let their rich go free! They even steal
The poor man's little for the rich man's weal!
Their feeble have a god their strong may flout!
They cut the land in pieces, fencing out
Their neighbors from the mother of all men!
When she is sick, they make her bear again
With medicines they give her with the seed!
All this is sacrilegious! Yet they heed
No word, and like a river in the spring
They flood the country, sweeping everything

Before them! 'Twas not many snows ago
They said that we might hunt our buffalo
In this our land forever. Now they come
To break that promise. Shall we cower, dumb?
Or shall we say: 'First kill us—here we stand!' "

He paused; then stooping to the mother-land,
He scraped a bit of dust and tossed it high.
Against the hollow everlasting sky
All watched it drifting, sifting back again
In utter silence. "So it is with men,"
Said Sitting Bull, his voice now low and tense;
"What better time, my friends, for going hence
Than when we have so many foes to kill?"

He ceased. As though they heard him speaking still,
The people listened; for he had a way
That seemed to mean much more than he could say
And over all the village cast a spell.
At length some warrior uttered in a yell
The common hate. 'Twas like the lean blue flash
That stabs a sultry hush before the crash
Of heaven-rending thunder and the loud
Assault of winds. Then fury took the crowd
And set it howling with the lust to slay.

The councillors were heard no more that day;
And from the moony hill tops all night long
The wolves gave answer to the battle-song,
And saw their valley hunting-grounds aflare
With roaring fires, and frenzied shadows there
That leaped and sang as wolves do, yet were men.

CHARLES BADGER CLARK JR. (1883–1957) ✳

Badger Clark lived as a boy in Deadwood, South Dakota, a gold rush town boasting five churches and twenty-six saloons. He later lived and ranched in Arizona near the Mexican border, where most of his poems were written. Many of his compositions became songs passed among the cowboys and are still recited or sung at cowboy poet gatherings. A number of classic cowboy songs such as "High Chin Bob," "A Cowboy's Prayer," and "Spanish Is the Lovin' Tongue" began as Badger Clark poems. Many songs lost their authors, or their titles were changed, as they passed from singer to singer. For cowboy poets, knowing how it feels "to sit a good horse" is as important as the musical line and work-earned metaphor.[33]

The Plainsmen

Men of the older, gentler soil,
    Loving the things that their fathers wrought—
Worn old fields of their fathers' toil,
    Scarred old hills where their fathers fought—
Loving their land for each ancient trace,
Like a mother dear for her wrinkled face,
    Such as they never can understand
    The way we have loved you, young, young land!

Born of a free, world-wandering race,
    Little we yearned o'er an oft-turned sod.
What did we care for the fathers' place,
    Having ours fresh from the hand of God?
Who feared the strangeness or wiles of you
When from the unreckoned miles of you,
    Thrilling the wind with a sweet command,
    Youth unto youth called, young, young land!

North, where the hurrying seasons changed
    Over great gray plains where the trails lay long,
Free as the sweeping Chinook we ranged,

Setting our days to a saddle song.
Through the icy challenge you flung to us,
Through your shy Spring kisses that clung to us,
    Following far as the rainbow spanned,
    Fiercely we wooed you, young, young land!

South, where the sullen black mountains guard
    Limitless, simmering lands of the sun,
Over blinding trails where the hoofs rang hard,
    Laughing or cursing, we rode and won.
Drunk with the virgin white fire of you,
Hotter than thirst was desire of you;
    Straight in our faces you burned your brand,
    Marking your chosen ones, young, young land.

When did we long for the sheltered gloom
    Of the older game with its cautious odds?
Gloried we always in sun and room,
    Spending our strength like the younger gods.
By the wild sweet ardor that ran in us,
By the pain that tested the man in us,
    By the shadowy springs and the glaring sand,
    You were our true-love, young, young land.

When the last free trail is a prim, fenced lane
    And our graves grow weeds through forgetful Mays,
Richer and statelier then you'll reign,
    Mother of men whom the world will praise.
And your sons will love you and sigh for you,
Labor and battle and die for you,
    But never the fondest will understand
    The way we loved you, young, young land.

✳

Roundup on the
Sherman Ranch,
Genesee, Kansas, 1902.

D. H. LAWRENCE (1885–1930) ✳ *The English author lived for a time in the Taos, New Mexico, arts colony that centered around the energies of Mabel Dodge Luhan. The Southwest inspired in Lawrence a group of poems that wed his lyric sense of the natural world with his concern for the subjugation of sensuality in what he saw as a dangerously rational age.*[34]

Men in New Mexico

Mountains blanket-wrapped
Round a white hearth of desert—

While the sun goes round
And round and round the desert,
The mountains never get up and walk about.
They can't, they can't wake.

They camped and went to sleep
In the last twilight
Of Indian gods;
And they can't wake.

Indians dance and run and stamp—
No good.
White men make gold-mines and the mountains unmake them
In their sleep.

The Indians laugh in their sleep
From fear,
Like a man when he sleeps and his sleep is over, and he can't wake up,
And he lies like a log and screams and his scream is silent
Because his body can't wake up;
So he laughs from fear, pure fear, in the grip of the sleep.

A dark membrane over the will, holding a man down
Even when the mind has flickered awake;
A membrane of sleep, like a black blanket.

We walk in our sleep, in this land,
Somnambulist wide-eyed afraid.
We scream for someone to wake us
And our scream is soundless in the paralysis of sleep,
And we know it.

The Penitentes lash themselves till they run with blood
In their efforts to come awake for one moment;
To tear the membrane of this sleep . . .
No good.

The Indians thought the white man would awake them . . .
And instead, the white men scramble asleep in the mountains,
And ride on horseback asleep forever through the desert,
And shoot one another, amazed and mad with somnambulism,
Thinking death will awaken something . . .
No good.

Born with a caul,
A black membrane over the face,
And unable to tear it,
Though the mind is awake.

Mountains blanket-wrapped
Round the ash-white hearth of the desert;
And though the sun leaps like a thing unleashed in the sky
They can't get up, they are under the blanket.

Taos.

HAZEL HALL (1886–1924) ✳   *One of Oregon's most celebrated poets of the 1920s, Hazel Hall was born in Minnesota, came to Portland as a child, and, after a bout with scarlet fever, used a wheelchair from the age of twelve. She took in fine needlework to support herself, while living confined to one upstairs room. Her poems appeared in distinguished literary journals of the time, and she was awarded the Young Poet's Prize from* Poetry *magazine in 1921. Her output was small—three volumes of poetry, one published posthumously.*[38]

The Listening Macaws

Many sewing days ago
I cross-stitched on a black satin bag
Two listening macaws.

They were perched on a stiff branch
With every stitch of their green tails,
Their blue wings, yellow breasts and sharply turned heads,
Alert and listening.

Picnic under a giant cactus near
Fort Thomas, Arizona, 1886.

Now sometimes on the edge of relaxation
My thought is caught back,
Like gathers along a gathering thread,
To the listening macaws;
And I am amazed at the futile energy
That has kept them,
Alert to the last stitch,
Listening into their black satin night.

White Day's Death

Light that streams into the grass
in white rain, light that fills a tree
With radiance like steel, like glass.
Makes me catch my breath to see.

Down, down it pours in cold sun, thinned
To web of crystal; streak on streak
It falls, chastening the wind
And making every small bird meek.

Farther into the ground's black space
Recedes earth's little warmth; earth grown
Unfecund, now is made a place
Of brittle dust and stone.

Silver filters through my eye
Until my very brain is lit
With the glitter of sterility
That is both grave and exquisite.

Late Sewing

There is nothing new in what is said
By either a needle or a thread:
Stitch, says a needle, *Stitch*, says the thread;
Stitch for the living; stitch for the dead;
All seams measure the same.

Garb for the living is light and gay.
While that for the dead is a shrouding grey,
But all things match on a later day
When little worm-stitches in the clay
Finish all seams the same.

For a Broken Needle

Even fine steel thinly made
To hold a raging thread,
Comes to lie with purple shade
In a dreaded bed.

All its chiseled length, its nice
Grip, its moving gleam
That was once like chips of ice
In a heated seam,

Are no more. It is fit
We should chant a strain
Of lament, then tumble it
Out into the rain.

STANLEY VESTAL (1887–1956) ✳

Vestal was novelist, poet, biographer, historian, writing teacher, and Rhodes scholar, and a Kansas plainsman who loved the Indian way of life and was twice adopted by Sioux chiefs. His best-known work was the biography Sitting Bull: Champion of the Sioux, *for which he interviewed a hundred old warriors who had fought in the Battle of the Little Bighorn. Vestal's ballads work within the conventions of the traditional English ballad form and hold, according to the author, "as strictly true to records of the Old West as the exigencies of balladry permit."*[36]

Kit Carson's Last Smoke

Kit Carson came to old Fort Lyons
Sick as he could be:
'Make me a bed of buffalo robes
On the floor in the corner,' says he;

'Make me bed of buffalo robes
Like we used along the trail;
I thought to ha' lived for a hundred year,
But my heart is beginning to fail;

'I ought to ha' lived for a hundred year,
But the strength in my legs is done;
I swelled the veins in them long ago
When the Blackfoot made me run.

'Take care of my children, *compadre*,
I've taken my last ride;
Bury my bones in good old Taos
By my dear Josephine's side.

'I leave you my Cross-J cattle,
My house and ranch, and the rest;
Tell Wiggins, and Tom, and the Carson men
That I always loved them best.

'Now cook me some first-rate doin's—
I'm tired of this sick man's feed;
A buffalo steak and a bowl of coffee
And a pipe are what I need.'

The Army doctor shook his head
And looked Kit in the eye:
'General, now, you ought to know,
If you eat that meal, you'll die!'

'I never was scairt of death,' says Kit;
His eye was cold and blue;
'I've faced it many's the time,' he said;
They knew his words were true.

'There war times when the Injuns bested me;
There war times when I run like sin;
But I never took fright of a square meal yet,
And it's too late now to begin.

'I'd ruther die on my pins,' Kit said,
'With the bull meat under my belt,
Than to die in my bed by inches
Like a beaver trapped for his pelt.'

They brought him a big thick buffalo steak:
He ate it every bite.
He smacked his lips when he drank his coffee,
And swore it tasted right.

'Will you have your meerschaum, General,
Or your Cheyenne calumet?
Will you have the pipe that Fremont gave,
Or what pipe shall we get?'

'Get me my old black clay, Sherrick;
Give me my old dudheen;
It has been over many a trail with me;
It has seen what I have seen.'

He packed the baccy in the bowl,
Inhaled the smoke so blue;
A happy smile spread o'er his face—
That face so bold and true.

He smoked the pipe out to the end
And brushed the ashes off.
Then Death (whose bullets could not kill)
Killed Kit with a little cough.

The ladies of that lonely post
They loved him one and all;
One gave her satin wedding-gown
To line his coffin-wall.

The ladies on that winter day
For love of one so brave
Pulled from their bonnets all the flowers
To strew upon his grave.

He was happy when he died,
And brave and true alive.
God send the West a many such
To make our country thrive!

ROBINSON JEFFERS (1887–1962) ✳

Jeffers was born in Pittsburgh. He and his wife settled in Carmel in 1914, where he built a home above the rocky coast and lived until his death. He published more than a dozen books of poetry—initially narrative and epic poems, including Tamar, Roan Stallion, *and* The Women at Point Sur. *His adaptation and translation of Euripides'* Medea, *produced in New York in 1947, won acclaim. Jeffers's later lyric poems mastered a richly musical long-lined free verse, profoundly informed by the coastal landscape. His prophetic themes grew increasingly bleak and bitter about humanity.*[37]

Rock and Hawk

Here is a symbol in which
Many high tragic thoughts
Watch their own eyes.

This gray rock, standing tall
On the headland, where the seawind
Lets no tree grow,

Earthquake-proved, and signatured
By ages of storms: on its peak
A falcon has perched.

I think, here is your emblem
To hang in the future sky;
Not the cross, not the hive,

But this; bright power, dark peace;
Fierce consciousness joined with final
Disinterestedness;

Life with calm death; the falcon's
Realist eyes and act
Married to the massive

Mysticism of stone,
Which failure cannot cast down
Nor success make proud.

The Purse-Seine

Our sardine fishermen work at night in the dark of the moon; daylight or moonlight
They could not tell where to spread the net, unable to see the phosphorescence of the shoals of fish.
They work northward from Monterey, coasting Santa Cruz; off New Year's Point or off Pigeon Point
The look-out man will see some lakes of milk-color light on the sea's night-purple; he points, and the helmsman
Turns the dark prow, the motorboat circles the gleaming shoal and drifts out her seine-net. They close the circle
And purse the bottom of the net, then with great labor haul it in.

I cannot tell you

How beautiful the scene is, and a little terrible, then, when the crowded fish

Know they are caught, and wildly beat from one wall to the other of their closing destiny the phosphorescent

Water to a pool of flame, each beautiful slender body sheeted with flame, like a live rocket

A comet's tail wake of clear yellow flame; while outside the narrowing

Floats and cordage of the net great sea-lions come up to watch, sighing in the dark; the vast walls of night

Stand erect to the stars.

           Lately I was looking from a night mountain-top

On a wide city, the colored splendor, galaxies of light: how could I help but recall the seine-net

Gathering the luminous fish? I cannot tell you how beautiful the city appeared, and a little terrible.

I thought, We have geared the machines and locked all together into interdependence; we have built the great cities; now

There is no escape. We have gathered vast populations incapable of free survival, insulated

From the strong earth, each person in himself helpless, on all dependent. The circle is closed, and the net

Is being hauled in. They hardly feel the cords drawing, yet they shine already. The inevitable mass-disasters

Will not come in our time nor in our children's, but we and our children

Must watch the net draw narrower, government take all powers—or revolution, and the new government

Take more than all, add to kept bodies kept souls—or anarchy, the mass-disasters.

           These things are Progress;

Do you marvel our verse is troubled or frowning, while it keeps its reason? Or it lets go, lets the mood flow

In the manner of the recent young men into mere hysteria, splintered gleams, crackled laughter. But they are quite wrong.

There is no reason for amazement: surely one always knew that cultures decay, and life's end is death.

The Coast-Road

A horseman high alone as an eagle on the spur of the mountain over Mirmas Canyon draws rein, looks down
At the bridge-builders, men, trucks, the power-shovels, the teeming end of the new coast-road at the mountain's base.
He sees the loops of the road go northward, headland beyond headland, into gray mist over Fraser's Point,
He shakes his fist and makes the gesture of wringing a chicken's neck, scowls and rides higher.

        I too
Believe that the life of men who ride horses, herders of cattle on the mountain pasture, plowers of remote
Rock-narrowed farms in poverty and freedom, is a good life. At the far end of those loops of road
Is what will come and destroy it, a rich and vulgar and bewildered civilization dying at the core,
A world that is feverishly preparing new wars, peculiarly vicious ones, and heavier tyrannies, a strangely
Missionary world, road-builder, wind-rider, educator, printer and picture-maker and broadcaster,
So eager, like an old drunken whore, pathetically eager to impose the seduction of her fled charms
On all that through ignorance or isolation might have escaped them. I hope the weathered horseman up yonder
Will die before he knows what this eager world will do to his children. More tough-minded men
Can repulse an old whore, or cynically accept her drunken kindnesses for what they are worth,
But the innocent and credulous are soon corrupted.

                                  Where is our
consolation? Beautiful beyond belief
The heights glimmer in the sliding cloud, the great bronze gorge-cut sides of the mountain tower up invincibly,
Not the least hurt by this ribbon of road carved on their sea-foot.

Vulture

I had walked since dawn and lay down to rest on a bare hillside
Above the ocean. I saw through half-shut eyelids a vulture wheeling high up in heaven,
And presently it passed again, but lower and nearer, its orbit narrowing, I understood then
That I was under inspection. I lay death-still and heard the flight-feathers
Whistle above me and make their circle and come nearer.

The overland stage route between Ogden and Helena crossing the Beaver Head River, 1871.

I could see the naked red head between the great wings

Bear downward staring. I said, "My dear bird, we are wasting time here.

These old bones will still work; they are not for you." But how beautiful he looked, gliding down

On those great sails; how beautiful he looked, veering away in the sea-light over the precipice. I tell you solemnly

That I was sorry to have disappointed him. To be eaten by that beak and become part of him, to share those wings and those eyes—

What a sublime end of one's body, what an enskyment; what a life after death.

GWENDOLEN HASTE (1889–) ❋   *Haste was born in Illinois and spent only ten or twelve years of her life in the West, mostly in Montana during her youth. Her best poems came from those experiences, and she enjoyed a national reputation as a poet during the 1930s and 1940s. She helped her father edit* The Scientific Farmer, *first in Lincoln, Nebraska, and later in Billings, Montana.*[38]

from Montana Wives

THE RANCH IN THE COULEE

He built the ranch house down a little draw,
So that he should have wood and water near.
The bluffs rose all around. She never saw
The arching sky, the mountains lifting clear;
But to the west the close hills fell away
And she could glimpse a few feet of the road.
The stage to Roundup went by every day,
Sometimes a rancher town-bound with his load,
An auto swirling dusty through the heat,
Or children trudging home on tired feet.

At first she watched it as she did her work,
A horseman pounding by gave her a thrill,
But then within her brain began to lurk
The fear that if she lingered from the sill
Someone might pass unseen. So she began
To keep the highroad always within sight,
And when she found it empty long she ran
And beat upon the pane and cried with fright.
The winter was the worst. When snow would fall
He found it hard to quiet her at all.

THE WIND
The cabin sits alone far up a hill
Where all the year the mournful wind blows shrill.

She used to tell him sometimes: "No one knows
How hard it is to listen while it blows."

He never touched a plow again, they say,
After he found her there, but went away.

And tenants wouldn't live upon the place
Because, the neighbors said, they saw her face

Pressed close against the little window-pane
Watching the twisting storm clouds in the rain,

And in the night time they could hear her cry
And moan and whimper if the gale was high.

So now through barren fields the great winds blow
Where fan weed and the purple wild pea grow.

They said she had no cause to die, but still
The wind was always blowing on that hill.

THOMAS HORNSBY FERRIL (1896–1988) ✳

The Empire Sofa

They could grow used to seeing bones
Of buffalo and sometime men,
They could grow strong on cracking dreams
Of gold to give them rest again,
They could pit happy years to come
Against the prairie's timeless length,
They had illusions that could calm
The frantic restlessness of strength.

But things like this they had to pass,
Sunk in the sand on the Arkansas,
This rosewood sofa that clutched the sun

Born in Denver, Ferril graduated from Colorado College and lived most of his life in the house where his father was born. He worked for the Great Western Sugar Company editing agricultural publications, as a drama critic for the Denver Times, *and in motion picture advertising. For many years he and his wife published* The Rocky Mountain Herald, *Denver's oldest weekly, founded in 1960. His first book,* High Passage, *won the Yale Younger Poets Award in 1926. He subsequently published five more volumes of lyric and narrative poems and wrote plays, musical productions, columns for* Harper's *magazine, and a collection of essays. Ferril is the most distinguished poet of the Rocky Mountain West; his poems accompany murals in the rotunda of the Colorado State Capitol building, and he is the subject of a 1982 documentary film titled* One Mile, Five-Foot-Ten.[39]

With every foot a gryphon's claw;
They saw it shining far ahead,
They turned to see it far behind,
And dreamed of men who dared to lose
The things they dared not hope to find.

One wagon whistled *Money Musk*,
Another chattered into laughter.
But no one spoke to anyone
About what they were going after;
An hour creaked by and dreams came back,
The wagons talked with even breath
And grew secure the more they passed
The more familiar forms of death.

Time of Mountains

So long ago my father led me to
The dark impounded orders of this canyon,
I have confused these rocks and waters with
My life, but not unclearly, for I know
What will be here when I am here no more.

I've moved in the terrible cries of the prisoned water,
And prodigious stillness where the water folds
Its terrible muscles over and under each other.

When you've walked a long time on the floor of a river,
And up the steps and into the different rooms,
You know where the hills are going, you can feel them,

Shoshone Canyon and Falls, Idaho Territory, 1867—1869.

The far blue hills dissolving in luminous water,
The solvent mountains going home to the oceans.
Even when the river is low and clear,
And the waters are going to sleep in the upper swales,
You can feel the particles of the shining mountains
Moping against your ankles toward the sea.

Forever the mountains are coming down and I stalk
Against them, cutting the channel with my shins,
With the lurch of the stiff spray cracking over my thighs;
I feel the bones of my back bracing my body,
And I push uphill behind the vertebrate fish
That lie uphill with their bony brains uphill
Meeting and splitting the mountains coming down.

I push uphill behind the vertebrate fish
That scurry uphill, ages ahead of me.
I stop to rest but the order still keeps moving;
I mark how long it takes an aspen leaf
To float in sight, pass me, and go downstream;
I watch a willow dipping and springing back
Like something that must be a water-clock,
Measuring mine against the end of mountains.

But if I go before these mountains go,
I'm unbewildered by the time of mountains,
I, who have followed life up from the sea
Into a black incision in this planet,
Can bring an end to stone infinitives.
I have held rivers to my eyes like lenses,
And rearranged the mountains at my pleasure,

As one might change the apples in a bowl,
And I have walked a dim unearthly prairie
From which these peaks have not yet blown away.

Blue-Stemmed Grass

There's blue-stemmed grass as far as I can see,
But when I take the blue-stemmed grass in hand,
And pull the grass apart, and speak the word
For every part, I do not understand
More than I understood of grass before.
"This part," I say, "is the straight untwisted awn,"
And "Here's the fourth glume of the sessile spikelet,"
And then I laugh out loud at what I've done.

I speak with reason to the blue-stemmed grass:
"This grass moves up through meadow beasts to men."
I weigh mechanical economies
Of meadow into flesh and back again.
I let the morning sun shine through my hand,
I trace the substance bloom and beast have given,
But I ask if phosphorus and nitrogen
Can make air through my lips mean hell or heaven.

All that the grass can make for any beast
Is here within my luminous hand of bone
And flesh and blood against the morning sun;
But I must listen alone, and you, alone,
Far children to be woven from green looms;
We move forever across meadows blowing,
But like no beast, we choke and cannot cry
When the grasses come, and when the grass is going.

JANET LEWIS (1899–) ✳ *Best known for her historical novels,* The Wife of Martin Guerre *and* The Trial of Sören Qvist, *Lewis first published poems when in her early twenties. Informed initially by American Indian songs and cultures, her poems later reflected the spare and precise work of the Imagists. She has also written children's books and libretti, and has taught at Stanford University and the University of California at Berkeley. She was married to the poet Yvor Winters. In her nineties, she continues to live and write in California.*[40]

A Grandmother Remembers

Ah, the cold, cold days
When we lived
On wintergreen berries and nuts,
On caraway seeds.

The deer went over the grass
With wet hooves
To the river to drink.

Their shadows passed
Our tent.

Snail Garden

This is the twilight hour of the morning
When the snails retreat over the wet grass
To their hidden world, when my dreams, retreating,
Leave me wondering what wisdom goes with them,
What hides in mouldering earth.

Softly they go, the snails,
Naked, unguarded, perceptive
Of the changing light, rejoicing
In their slow progress from leaf to stem,
From stem to deeper darkness.
Smoothness delights them.

What do they hear? The air above them
Is full of the sharp cries of birds.
Do they see? The lily bud,
Three feet above the soil on its leafy stalk,
Is known to them at midnight
As if it were a lighthouse. Before sunrise
They have gnawed it half in two.
Toothless mouths, blind mouths
Have turned the leaf of the hollyhock to lace,
And cut the stem of the nasturtium
Neatly, just below the blossom.

The classic shell, cunningly arched, and strong
Against the hazards of the grassy world
Is nothing before the power of my intention.
The larks, also, have had their fun,
Crashing that coiled shell on stone,
Guiltless in their freedom.

But I have taken sides in the universe.
I have killed the snail that lay on the morning leaf,
Not grudging greatly the nourishment it took
Out of my abundance,
Chard, periwinkle, capucine,
Occasional lily bud,

But I have begun my day with death,
Death given, death to be received.
I have stepped into the dance;
I have greeted at daybreak
That necessary angel, that other.

YVOR WINTERS (1900–1968) ✳ *Born in Chicago, Winters studied at the Universities of Chicago and Colorado and received a Ph.D. from Stanford, where he served as an influential teacher from 1928 until his death. He was known during his lifetime as a conservative antimodernist critic who held to traditional prosody and the idea of art "as an act of moral judgement." His student Philip Levine has described Winters's poems as "placed perfectly in the moral and physical landscape of California, poems unlike anything that existed in America until he wrote them."[41]*

John Sutter

I was the patriarch of the shining land,
Of the blond summer and metallic grain;
Men vanished at the motion of my hand,
And when I beckoned they would come again.

The earth grew dense with grain at my desire;
The shade was deepened at the springs and streams;
Moving in dust that clung like pillared fire,
The gathering herds grew heavy in my dreams.

Across the mountains, naked from the heights,
Down to the valley broken settlers came,
And in my houses feasted through the nights,
Rebuilt their sinews and assumed a name.

✳ Panning for gold near Virginia
City, Montana, 1871.

In my clear rivers my own men discerned
The motive for the ruin and the crime—
Gold heavier than earth, a wealth unearned,
Loot, for two decades, from the heart of Time.

Metal, intrinsic value, deep and dense,
Preanimate, inimitable, still,
Real, but an evil with no human sense,
Dispersed the mind to concentrate the will.

Grained by alchemic change, the human kind
Turned from themselves to rivers and to rocks;
With dynamite broke metal unrefined;
Measured their moods by geologic shocks.

With knives they dug the metal out of stone;
Turned rivers back, for gold through ages piled,
Drove knives to hearts, and faced the gold alone;
Valley and river ruined and reviled;

Reviled and ruined me, my servant slew,
Strangled him from the figtree by my door.
When they had done what fury bade them do,
I was a cursing beggar, stripped and sore.

What end impersonal, what breathless age,
Incontinent of quiet and of years,
What calm catastrophe will yet assuage
This final drouth of penitential tears?

To the Holy Spirit

from a deserted graveyard in the Salinas Valley

Immeasurable haze:
The desert valley spreads
Up golden river-beds
As if in other days.
Trees rise and thin away,
And past the trees, the hills,
Pure line and shade of dust,
Bear witness to our wills:
We see them, for we must;
Calm in deceit, they stay.

High noon returns the mind
Upon its local fact:
Dry grass and sand; we find
No vision to distract.
Low in the summer heat,
Naming old graves, are stones
Pushed here and there, the seat
Of nothing, and the bones
Beneath are similar:
Relics of lonely men,
Brutal and aimless, then,
As now, irregular.

These are thy fallen sons,
Thou whom I try to reach.
Thou whom the quick eye shuns,
Thou dost elude my speech.

Yet when I go from sense
And trace thee down in thought,
I meet thee, then, intense,
And know thee as I ought.
But thou art mind alone,
And I, alas, am bound
Pure mind to flesh and bone,
And flesh and bone to ground.

These had no thought: at most
Dark faith and blinding earth.
Where is the trammeled ghost?
Was there another birth?
Only one certainty
Beside thine unfleshed eye,
Beside the spectral tree,
Can I discern: these die.
All of this stir of age,
Though it elude my sense
Into what heritage
I know not, seems to fall,
Quiet beyond recall,
Into irrelevance.

ANONYMOUS (c. 1908) ✳   *In 1908 N. Howard "Jack" Thorp printed in Estancia, New Mexico, a small collection of
cowboy songs he had collected on the range. Scholars have traced the origins of "Cow
Boy's Lament" to the early 1700s. There are hundreds of versions of the text, all dealing
with the death of a sinner dying in a street or on a barroom floor. These songs, and new
ones, continue to be adapted by contemporary cowboy poets and singers.*[42]

Cow Boy's Lament

'Twas once in my saddle I used to be happy
    'twas once in my saddle I used to be gay
But I first took to drinking, then to gambling
    A shot from a six-shooter took my life away.

My curse let it rest, let it rest on the fair one
    Who drove me from friends that I loved and from home
Who told me she loved me, just to deceive me
    My curse rest upon her, wherever she roam.

Oh she was fair, O she was lovely
    The belle of the Village the fairest of all
But her heart was as cold as the snow on the mountains
    She gave me up for the glitter of gold.

I arrived in Galveston in old Texas
    Drinking and gambling I went to give o'er
But, I met with a Greaser and my life he has finished
    Home and relations I ne'er shall see more.

Cattle roundup, Arizona Territory, 1896—1899.

Send for my father, Oh send for my mother
 Send for the surgeon to look at my wounds
But I fear it is useless I feel I am dying
 I'm a young cow-boy cut down in my bloom.

Farewell my friends, farewell my relations
 My earthly career has cost me sore
The cow-boy ceased talking, they knew he was dying
 His trials on earth, forever were o'er.

CHOR.
Beat your drums lightly, play your fifes merrily
 Sing your death march as you bear me along
Take me to the grave yard, lay the sod o'er me
 I'm a young cow-boy and know I've done wrong.

Educated Feller

We were camped upon the plains near the Cimmaron
When along came a stranger and stopped to argue some
He was a well educated feller his talk just come in herds
And astonished all the punchers with his jaw breaking words.

He had a well worn saddle and we thought it kind'er strange
That he didn't know much about working on the range
He'd been at work he said, up near the Santa Fe
And was cutting cross country to strike the 7 D

Had to quit an outfit up near Santa Fe
Had some trouble with the boss, just what he didn't say
Said his horse was 'bout to give out would like to get another
If the punchers wouldn't mind and it wasn't too much bother.

Yes we'll give you a horse, he's just as sound as a bun
They quickly grabbed a lariat and roped the Zebra Dun.
Turned him over to the stranger
Then they waited to see the fun.

Old Dunny stands right still not seeming to know
Until the stranger's ready and a fixing up to go
When he goes into the saddle old Dunny leaves the earth
He travels right straight up for all he was worth.

But he sits up in his saddle just pullin his mustach
Just like some summer boarder a waiting for his hash
Old Dunny pitched and bauled and had wall eyed fits
His hind feet perpendicular his front ones in his bits.

With one foot in the stirrup, he just thought it fun
The other leg around the saddle horn the way he rode old Dun.
He spurred him in the shoulder and hit him as he whirled
Just to show these flunky punchers the best rider in the world.

The boss says to him, you needn't go on
If you can use the rope like you rode old Dun.
You've a job with me if you want to come
You're the man I've been looking for since the year one.

I can sling the rope, an' I'm not very slow
I can catch nine times out of ten for any kind of dough
Now there's one thing and a sure thing I've learned since I was born
That all these educated fellows are not green horns.

List all you Californ'y boys
  And open wide your ears
For now we start across the plains
  With a herd of mules and steers.
Now bear it in mind before you start
  That you'll eat jerked beef not ham
And antelope steak oh cuss the stuff
  It often proves a sham.

You cannot find a stick of wood
  On all this prairie wide
Whene'er you eat you've got to stand
  Or sit on some old bull hide.
It's fun to cook with Buffalo Chips
  Or Mesquite green as corn
If I'd once known what I know now
  I'd have gone around Cape Horn.

The women have the hardest time
  Who emigrate by land
For when they cook out in the wind
  They're sure to burn their hands.
Then they scold their husbands 'round
  Get mad and spill the tea
I'd have thanked my stars if they'd not come out
  Upon this bleak prairie.

[*]Thorp attributes this song to Kate Childs, otherwise known as
Montana Kate, written in about 1869. He first heard it sung by
Sam Murphy at Horse Head Crossing on the Peace (or Pease?) River
in 1900.

Most every night we put out guards
　　To keep the Indians off
When night comes round some heads will ache
　　And some begin to cough.
To be deprived of help at night
　　You know it's mighty hard
But every night there's someone sick
　　To get rid of standing guard.

Then they're always talking of what they've got
　　And what they're going to do
Some will say they are content
　　For I've got as much as you.
Others will say I'll buy or sell
　　And damned if I care which
Others will say boys buy him out
　　For he doesn't own a stitch.

Old rawhide shoes are Hell on corns
　　While tramping through the sands
And driving a Jackass by the tail
　　Damn the overland.
I would as lief be on a raft at sea
　　And there at once be lost
John let's leave this poor old mule
　　We'll never get him across.

ANONYMOUS (EARLY 1900s) ✳

The early 1900s were a time of transition on the U.S.–Mexico border. Tension was building toward the Mexican Revolution. Reports about lynchings of Mexicans in Texas caused anti-American riots in Mexico City. The period is marked by a flourishing of corridos, or border ballads. No other corrido has been more widely known among Mexicans throughout the U.S. than "El Corrido de Gregorio Cortez." On June 12, 1901, Cortez shot and killed Sheriff Brack Morris seconds after the sheriff had shot Cortez's brother. The sheriff was trying to arrest the brothers for a crime they had not committed. Cortez fled toward the Rio Grande, walked more than a hundred miles, and rode another four hundred, eluding, temporarily, the hundreds of men trying to capture him.[43]

El Corrido de Gregorio Cortez

In the county of El Carmen
A great misfortune befell;
The Major Sheriff is dead;
Who killed him no one can tell.

At two in the afternoon
In half an hour or less,
They knew that the man who killed
Had been Gregorio Cortez.

They let loose the bloodhound dogs;
They followed him from afar.
But trying to catch Cortez
Was like following a star.

All the rangers of the county
Were flying, they rode so hard;
What they wanted was to get
The thousand-dollar reward.

And in the county of Kiansis
They cornered him after all;
Though they were more than three hundred
He leaped out of their corral.

Then the Major Sheriff said,
As if he was going to cry,
"Cortez, hand over your weapons;
We want to take you alive."

Then said Gregorio Cortez,
And his voice was like a bell,
"You will never get my weapons
Till you put me in a cell."

Then said Gregorio Cortez,
With his pistol in his hand,
"Ah, so many mounted Rangers
Just to take one Mexican!"

(Translated by Américo Paredes)

THEODORE ROETHKE (1908–1963) ✳

Born in Michigan, Roethke was educated at the University of Michigan and at Harvard. His father grew flowers, and Roethke's early experiences in greenhouses shaped both the imagery and the themes of his poetry. He published six books of poems; The Waking *won the 1953 Pulitzer Prize. He taught at the University of Washington. Roethke's metaphysical concerns found correspondence with the natural world. His work greatly influenced other writers, particularly those of the Pacific Northwest.*[44]

Moss-Gathering

To loosen with all ten fingers held wide and limber
And lift up a patch, dark-green, the kind for lining cemetery baskets,
Thick and cushiony, like an old-fashioned doormat,
The crumbling small hollow sticks on the underside mixed with roots,
And wintergreen berries and leaves still stuck to the top,—
That was moss-gathering.
But something always went out of me when I dug loose those carpets
Of green, or plunged to my elbows in the spongy yellowish moss of the marshes:
And afterwards I always felt mean, jogging back over the logging road,
As if I had broken the natural order of things in that swampland;
Disturbed some rhythm, old and of vast importance,
By pulling off flesh from the living planet;
As if I had committed, against the whole scheme of life, a desecration.

Meditation at Oyster River

I
Over the low, barnacled, elephant-colored rocks,
Come the first tide-ripples, moving, almost without sound, toward me,
Running along the narrow furrows of the shore, the rows of dead clam shells;
Then a runnel behind me, creeping closer,
Alive with tiny striped fish, and young crabs climbing in and out of the water.

No sound from the bay. No violence.
Even the gulls quiet on the far rocks,
Silent, in the deepening light,
Their cat-mewing over,
Their child-whimpering.

At last one long undulant ripple,
Blue-black from where I am sitting,
Makes almost a wave over the barrier of small stones,
Slapping lightly against a sunken log.
I dabble my toes in the brackish foam sliding forward,
Then retire to a rock higher up on the cliff-side.
The wind slackens, light as a moth fanning a stone:
A twilight wind, light as a child's breath
Turning not a leaf, not a ripple.
The dew revives on the beach-grass;
The salt-soaked wood of a fire crackles;
A fish raven turns on its perch (a dead tree in the rivermouth),
Its wings catching a last glint of the reflected sunlight.

2
The self persists like a dying star,
In sleep, afraid. Death's face rises afresh,
Among the shy beasts, the deer at the salt-lick,
The doe with its sloped shoulders loping across the highway,
The young snake, poised in green leaves, waiting for its fly,
The hummingbird, whirring from quince-blossom to morning-glory—
With these I would be.
And with water: the waves coming forward, without cessation,
The waves, altered by sand-bars, beds of kelp, miscellaneous driftwood,
Topped by cross-winds, tugged at by sinuous undercurrents
The tide rustling in, sliding between the ridges of stone,
The tongues of water, creeping in, quietly.

3
In this hour,
In this first heaven of knowing,
The flesh takes on the pure poise of the spirit,
Acquires, for a time, the sandpiper's insouciance,
The hummingbird's surety, the kingfisher's cunning—
I shift on my rock, and I think:
Of the first trembling of a Michigan brook in April,
Over a lip of stone, the tiny rivulet:
And that wrist-thick cascade tumbling from a cleft rock,
Its spray holding a double rain-bow in early morning,
Small enough to be taken in, embraced, by two arms,—
Or the Tittebawasee, in the time between winter and spring,
When the ice melts along the edges in early afternoon.
And the midchannel begins cracking and heaving from the pressure beneath,
The ice piling high against the iron-bound spiles,
Gleaming, freezing hard again, creaking at midnight—
And I long for the blast of dynamite,
The sudden sucking roar as the culvert loosens its debris of branches and sticks,
Welter of tin cans, pails, old bird nests, a child's shoes riding a log,
As the piled ice breaks away from the battered spiles,
And the whole river begins to move forward, its bridges shaking.

4
Now, in this waning light,
I rock with the motion of morning;
In the cradle of all that is,
I'm lulled into half-sleep
By the lapping of water,
Cries of the sandpiper.

Water's my will, and my way,
And the spirit runs, intermittently,
In and out of the small waves,
Runs with the intrepid shorebirds—
How graceful the small before danger!

In the first of the moon,
All's a scattering,
A shining.

In a Dark Time

In a dark time, the eye begins to see,
I meet my shadow in the deepening shade;
I hear my echo in the echoing wood—
A lord of nature weeping to a tree.
I live between the heron and the wren,
Beasts of the hill and serpents of the den.

What's madness but nobility of soul
At odds with circumstance? The day's on fire!
I know the purity of pure despair,
My shadow pinned against a sweating wall.
That place among the rocks—is it a cave,
Or winding path? The edge is what I have.

A steady storm of correspondences!
A night flowing with birds, a ragged moon,
And in broad day the midnight come again!
A man goes far to find out what he is—
Death of the self in a long, tearless night,
All natural shapes blazing unnatural light.

Dark, dark my light, and darker my desire.
My soul, like some heat-maddened summer fly,
Keeps buzzing at the sill. Which I is *I?*
A fallen man, I climb out of my fear.
The mind enters itself, and God the mind,
And one is One, free in the tearing wind.

CZESLAW MILOSZ (1911–) ❋ *Polish poet, essayist, and novelist Milosz won the 1980 Nobel Prize for literature. During World War II he fought in the resistance; after several years of diplomatic service, he cut his ties with the government and became an exile. He has lived and taught in Berkeley, California, since 1960. He was the first Slavic poet to hold the Charles Eliot Norton professorship at Harvard, from which lectures came his influential work on poetics and politics,* The Witness of Poetry. *Milosz continues to write in Polish, working with cotranslators (most frequently Robert Hass) to adapt the poems to English. Milosz has placed each of the poems included here in California. "There are many cities and countries in my mind," Milosz has written about his Berkeley life, "but they all stand in relation to the one which surrounds me every day."* [45]

To Robinson Jeffers

If you have not read the Slavic poets
so much the better. There's nothing there
for a Scotch-Irish wanderer to seek. They lived in a childhood
prolonged from age to age. For them, the sun
was a farmer's ruddy face, the moon peeped through a cloud
and the Milky Way gladdened them like a birch-lined road.
They longed for the Kingdom which is always near,
always right at hand. Then, under apple trees
angels in homespun linen will come parting the boughs
and at the white kolkhoz tablecloth
cordiality and affection will feast (falling to the ground at times).

And you are from surf-rattled skerries. From the heaths
where burying a warrior they broke his bones
so he could not haunt the living. From the sea night
which your forefathers pulled over themselves, without a word.
Above your head no face, neither the sun's nor the moon's,
only the throbbing of galaxies, the immutable
violence of new beginnings, of new destruction.

All your life listening to the ocean. Black dinosaurs
wade where a purple zone of phosphorescent weeds
rises and falls on the waves as in a dream. And Agamemnon
sails the boiling deep to the steps of the palace
to have his blood gush onto marble. Till mankind passes
and the pure and stony earth is pounded by the ocean.

Thin-lipped, blue-eyed, without grace or hope,
before God the Terrible, body of the world.
Prayers are not heard. Basalt and Granite.
Above them, a bird of prey. The only beauty.

What have I to do with you? From footpaths in the orchards,
from an untaught choir and shimmers of a monstrance,
from flower beds of rue, hills by the rivers, books
in which a zealous Lithuanian announced brotherhood, I come.
Oh, consolations of mortals, futile creeds.

And yet you did not know what I know. The earth teaches
More than does the nakedness of elements. No one with impunity
gives to himself the eyes of a god. So brave, in a void,
you offered sacrifices to demons: there were Wotan and Thor,
the screech of Erinyes in the air, the terror of dogs
when Hekate with her retinue of the dead draws near.

Better to carve suns and moons on the joints of crosses
as was done in my district. To birches and firs
give feminine names. To implore protection
against the mute and treacherous might
than to proclaim, as you did, an inhuman thing.

Berkeley, 1963

It Was Winter

Winter came as it does in this valley.
After eight dry months rain fell
And the mountains, straw-colored, turned green for a while.
In the canyons where gray laurels
Graft their stony roots to granite,
Streams must have filled the dried-up creek beds.
Ocean winds churned the eucalyptus trees,
And under clouds torn by a crystal of towers
Prickly lights were glowing on the docks.

This is not a place where you sit under a café awning
On a marble piazza, watching the crowd,
Or play the flute at a window over a narrow street
While children's sandals clatter in the vaulted entryway.

They heard of a land, empty and vast,
Bordered by mountains. So they went, leaving behind crosses
Of thorny wood and traces of campfires.
As it happened, they spent winter in the snow of a mountain pass,
And drew lots and boiled the bones of their companions;
And so afterward a hot valley where indigo could be grown
Seemed beautiful to them. And beyond, where fog
Heaved into shoreline coves, the ocean labored.

Sleep: rocks and capes will lie down inside you,
War councils of motionless animals in a barren place,
Basilicas of reptiles, a frothy whiteness.
Sleep on your coat, while your horse nibbles grass
And an eagle gauges a precipice.

When you wake up, you will have the parts of the world.
West, an empty conch of water and air.
East, always behind you, the voided memory of snow-covered fir.
And extending from your outspread arms
Nothing but bronze grasses, north and south.

We are poor people, much afflicted.
We camped under various stars,
Where you dip water with a cup from a muddy river
And slice your bread with a pocketknife.
This is the place; accepted, not chosen.
We remembered that there were streets and houses where we came from,
So there had to be houses here, a saddler's signboard,
A small veranda with a chair. But empty, a country where
The thunder beneath the rippled skin of the earth,
The breaking waves, a patrol of pelicans, nullified us.
As if our vases, brought here from another shore,
Were the dug-up spearheads of some lost tribe
Who fed on lizards and acorn flour.

And here I am walking the eternal earth.
Tiny, leaning on a stick.
I pass a volcanic park, lie down at a spring,
Not knowing how to express what is always and everywhere:
The earth I cling to is so solid
Under my breast and belly that I feel grateful

For every pebble, and I don't know whether
It is my pulse or the earth's that I hear,
When the hems of invisible silk vestments pass over me,
Hands, wherever they have been, touch my arm,
Or small laughter, once, long ago over wine,
With lanterns in the magnolias, for my house is huge.

Berkeley, 1964

MAY SWENSON (1913–1989) ✳ *Swenson was born in Utah to a Mormon family. She worked as a journalist, editor, ghostwriter, and poet-in-residence, living after 1949 in New York. The western influence remained important in her poetry. Eleven volumes of her poems were published during her life, winning her many honors and awards, including the Bollingen Prize in Poetry and a MacArthur Fellowship. She translated the work of Tomas Tranströmer and other Swedish poets.*[46]

Bison Crossing Near Mt. Rushmore

There is our herd of cars stopped,
staring respectfully at the line of bison crossing.
One big-fronted bull nudges his cow into a run.
She and her calf are first to cross.
In swift dignity the dark-coated caravan sweeps through
the gap our cars leave in the two-way stall
on the road to the Presidents.
The polygamous bulls guarding their families from the rear,
the honey-brown calves trotting head-to-hip
by their mothers—who are lean and muscled as bulls,
with chin tassels and curved horns—

all leap the road like a river, and run.

  The strong and somber remnant of western freedom
disappears into the rough grass of the draw,
around the point of the mountain.

  The bison, orderly, disciplined by the prophet-faced,
heavy-headed fathers, threading the pass
of our awestruck stationwagons, Airstreams and trailers,
if in dread of us give no sign,
go where their leaders twine them, over the prairie.

  And we keep to our line,
staring, stirring, revving idling motors, moving
each behind the other, herdlike, where the highway leads.

Weather

I hope they never get a rope on you, weather.
I hope they never put a bit in your mouth.
I hope they never pack your snorts
into an engine or make you wear wheels.

I hope the astronauts will always have to wait
till you get off the prairie
because your kick is lethal,
your temper worse than the megaton.

I hope your harsh mane will grow forever,
and blow where it will,
that your slick hide will always shiver
and flick down your bright sweat.

The Three Brothers, Yosemite, California.

Reteach us terror, weather,
with your teeth on our ships,
your hoofs on our houses,
your tail swatting our planes down like flies.

Before they make a grenade of our planet
I hope you'll come like a comet,
oh mustang—fire-eyes, upreared belly—
bust the corral and stomp us to death.

WILLIAM STAFFORD (1914–1993) ✳ *Born in Kansas, Stafford was educated in Kansas, Wisconsin, and Iowa. A conscientious objector to war, he served in work camps from 1942 to 1946, fighting forest fires and building trails and roads. He moved to Oregon in 1948 and taught for many years at Lewis and Clark College in Portland. He was the first Oregon poet to win the National Book Award. His book on poetics,* Writing the Australian Crawl, *has been influential.*[47]

Montana Eclogue

I
After the fall drive, the last
horseman humps down the trail south;
High Valley turns into a remote, still cathedral.
Stone Creek in its low bank turns calmly
through the trampled meadow. The one scouting
thunderhead above Long Top hangs to watch,
ready for its reinforcement due in October.

Logue, the man who always closes down the camp,
is left all alone at Cedar Lake, where
he is leisurely but busy, pausing to glance across
the water toward Winter Peak. The bunkhouse
will be boarded up, the cookshack barricaded
against bears, the corral gates lashed shut.
Whatever winter needs, it will have to find
for itself, all the slow months the wind owns.

From that shore below the mountain the water
darkens; the whole surface of the lake livens,
and, upward, high miles of pine tops bend where a storm

walks the country. Deeper and deeper, autumn
floods in. Nothing can hold against that current
the aspens feel. And Logue, by being there, suddenly
carries for us everything that we can load on him,
we who have stopped indoors and let our faces
forget how storms come: that lonely man works for us.

II
Far from where we are, air owns those ranches
our trees hardly hear of, open places
braced against cold hills. Mornings, that
news hits the leaves like rain, and we
stop everything time brings, and freeze that one,
open, great, real thing—the world's gift: day.

Up there, air like an axe drops, near timberline,
the clear-cut miles the marmots own. We
try to know, all deep, all sharp, even while
busy here, that other: gripped in a job,
aimed steady at a page, or riffled by distractions,
we break free into that world of the farthest coast—air.

We glimpse that last storm when the wolves
get the mountains back, when our homes will flicker
bright, then dull, then old; and the trees
will advance, knuckling their roots or lying in
windrows to match the years. We glimpse
a crack that begins to run down the wall,
and like a blanket over the window at night
that world is with us and those wolves are here.

✳
Interior of Sawtell's Ranch,
Fremont County, Idaho Territory, 1872.
PHOTO: JACKSON.

Up there, ready to be part of what comes, the high lakes
lie in their magnificent beds; but men,
great as their heroes are, live by their deeds
only as a pin of shadow in a cavern their thought
gets lost in. We pause; we stand where
we are meant to be, waver as foolish as
we are, tell our lies with all the beautiful grace
an animal has when it runs—

Citizen, step back from the fire and let night
have your head: suddenly you more than hear
what is true so abruptly that God is cold:—
winter is here. What no one saw, has
come. Then everything the sun approved could
really fail? Shed from your back, the years
fall one by one, and nothing that comes
will be your fault. You breathe a few breaths
free at the thought: things can come so great
that your part is too small to count,
if winter can come.

Logue brings us all that. Earth took
the old saints, who battered their hearts,
met arrows, or died by the germs God sent;
but Logue, by being alone and occurring to us,
carries us forward a little,
and on his way out for the year will
stand by the shore and see winter in,
the great, repeated lesson every year.

A storm bends by that shore and
one flake at a time teaches grace,
even to stone.

Allegiances

It is time for all the heroes to go home
if they have any, time for all of us common ones
to locate ourselves by the real things
we live by.

Far to the north, or indeed in any direction,
strange mountains and creatures have always lurked—
elves, goblins, trolls, and spiders:—we
encounter them in dread and wonder,

But once we have tasted far streams, touched the gold,
found some limit beyond the waterfall,
a season changes, and we come back, changed
but safe, quiet, grateful.

Suppose an insane wind holds all the hills
while strange beliefs whine at the traveler's ears,
we ordinary beings can cling to the earth and love
where we are, sturdy for common things.

THOMAS MCGRATH (1916–1990) ✳ *McGrath was born on a North Dakota farm. He studied at the University of
North Dakota and at Oxford. He began writing in the thirties, and his work
reflects his identification both with the West and with the radical labor
movement. While working as a scriptwriter, he was blacklisted for his political
convictions. His great work is an epistolary lyric several hundred pages long,
"Letter to an Imaginary Friend," that is at once an autobiography and an
elegiac exploration of western American history, politics, and economics.*[48]

from Letter to an Imaginary Friend

from PART ONE, VII. 2

. . . All that winter, in the black cold, the buzz-saw screamed and whistled,
And the rhyming hills complained. In the noontime stillness,
Thawing our frozen beans at the raw face of a fire,
We heard the frost-bound tree-boles booming like cannon,
A wooden thunder, snapping the chains of the frost.

Those were the last years of the Agrarian City
City of swapped labor
Communitas
Circle of warmth and work
Frontier's end and last wood-chopping bee
The last collectivity stamping its feet in the cold.

So, with the moss on our backs and it snowing inside our skulls,
In a gale like a mile-high window of breaking glass
We snaked out the down ones, snatching the deadfalls clean
And fed them into the buzzsaw.
                     The Frenchman's, it was.
A little guy, quick as a fart and no nicer,
Captain of our industry.

                              Had, for his company
The weedy sons of midnight enterprise:
Stump-jumpers and hog-callers from the downwind counties
The noonday mopus and the coffee guzzling Swedes
Prairie mules
Moonfaced Irish from up-country farms
Sand-hill cranes
And lonesome deadbeats from a buckbrush parish.

So, worked together. Fed the wood to the saw
That had more gaps than teeth. Sweated, and froze
In the dead-still days, as clear as glass, with the biting
Acetylene of the cold cutting in through the daylight,
And the badman trees snapping out of the dusk
Their icy pistols.
                        So, worked, the peddlers pack of us
Hunched in the cold with the Frenchman raging around us
A monsoon of fury, a wispy apocalypse, scolding
Cursing and pleading, whipping us into steam,
And we warmed in each other's work, contestants of winter,
We sawed up the summer into stove-length rounds—
Chunks of pure sunlight made warmer by our work.
And did we burn?
We burned with a cold flame.
And did we freeze?
We froze in bunches of five.
And did we complain?
We did, we did, we did.

I turn to the slope
That lifts to the bench, taking a path that the rabbits broke
In their moon-crazed rambles.

I grope for handholds in the buckbrush clumps,
I thumb the horny gooseberry brittle: stiff in his winter
Dress

—grab on and climb.

A rime of icy crystal
Glitters around my going like sun-maddened precious stones!

A step; a half-step, and a step more. I finally make it
Over the shallow lip and stand on the low plateau:
Here's Tommy Comelately to pore over the bones
Another time.

And what's here—on the little bluff
Over the little river?

A way station, merely;
A half-way house for the Indian dead—analphabetic
Boneyard . . .

It was here the Sioux had a camp on the long trail
Cutting the loops of the rivers from beyond the Missouri and Mandan
East: toward Big Stone Lake and beyond to the Pipestone Quarry,
The place of peace.

A backwoods road of a trail, no tribal
Superhighway; for small bands only. Coming and going
They pitched camp here a blink of an eye ago.

It's all gone now—nothing to show for it.

Skulls
Under the permanent snow of time no wind will lift
Nor shift . . .

—these drifting bones have entered the rock forever . . .

Chirachua Apache Prisoners, including Geronimo (first row third from right), Arizona, 1886.   PHOTO: J. MACDONALD.

And all done in the wink of an eye! Why my grandmother saw them—
And saw the last one perhaps: ascending the little river
On the spring high water in a battered canoe.
                                        Stole one of her chickens
(Herself in the ark of the soddy with the rifle cocked but not arguing)
Took the stolen bird and disappeared into history.

And my father, a boy at Fort Ransom, saw them each spring and fall—
Teepees strung on the fallow field where he herded cattle.
Made friends and swapped ponies with a boy his own age—
And in the last Indian scare spent a week in the old fort:
All the soddies abandoned, then.
                        Wounded Knee—
The last fight—must have been at that time.
                                        And now
All: finished.
            South Dakota has stolen the holy
Bones of Sitting Bull to make a tourist attraction!

From Indians we learned a toughness and a strength; and we gained
A freedom: by taking theirs: but a real freedom: born
From the wild and open land our grandfathers heroically stole.
But we took a wound at Indian hands: a part of our soul scabbed over:
We learned the pious and patriotic art of extermination
And no uneasy conscience where the man's skin was the wrong
Color; or his vowels shaped wrong; or his haircut; or his country possessed of
Oil; or holding the wrong place on the map—whatever
The master race wants it will find good reasons for having.

✳

The wind lifts and drones on the hill where a file of whispering
Snow wears at the bench-slope, rattling the sleet-stiff buckbrush,

And a train of cloud piles down from the high north,
Hiding the sun.
                          The day collapses toward evening.
                                                    Cold,
I turn from the bone-white field and drive my feet toward home.

In the thickening early gloom the first of the night hunting
Begins.
            On a quickening wing, a Great Snowy Owl,
Pure as a mile of Christmas, sifts and seethes down the sky,
And the shy and hiding rabbit hears and turns his white softness
To stone.
            Tranced, fear serves and saves him.
                                      The owl steers over,
Swings out on a spur of wind, swerves in his search and is gone.

Snow on the wind.
                    First farmlight.
                              In the downriver darkness.
A fox barks.
            Once.
                                Again.
                                    Silence and snow . . .
—And the fisherman still alive in the future in Skyros!
                                            (But dead
Now and forever.)
              In the boneyard . . .
                              Simulacra . . .
                                        The Indian is the first
Wound.

DENISE LEVERTOV (1923–) ✳

Levertov, born in England, has lived in the United States since 1948 and has published twenty-two books, as well as working as a political activist against the Vietnam War and the proliferation of nuclear arms. Often associated with Black Mountain poetics, she argued, along with Robert Creeley and Charles Olson, for organic form over the traditional metrical line, believing that "there is a form in all things" that the poem can reveal. She has taught at many universities, most recently at Stanford. Levertov has lived in Seattle since the late 1980s, and the presence of Mount Rainier has become a spiritual emblem in her recent work.[49]

What It Could Be

Uranium, with which we know
only how to destroy,

lies always under
the most sacred lands—

Australia, Africa, America,
wherever it's found is found an oppressed
ancient people who knew
long before white men found and named it
that there under their feet

under rock, under mountain, deeper
than deepest watersprings, under
the vast deserts familiar
inch by inch to their children

lay a great power.
          And they knew the folly
of wresting, wrestling, ravaging from the earth
that which it kept
          so guarded.

Now, now, now at this instant,
men are gouging lumps of that power, that presence,
out of the tortured planet the ancients
say is our mother.
                              Breaking the doors
of her sanctum, tearing the secret
out of her flesh.

But left to lie, its metaphysical weight
might in a million years have proved
benign, its true force being to be
a clue to righteousness—
showing forth
the human power
not to kill, to choose
not to kill: to transcend
the dull force of our weight and will;

that known profound presence, *un*touched,
the sign
providing witness,
                    occasion,
                    ritual
for the continuing act of
*non*violence, of passionate
reverence, active love.

Settling

I was welcomed here—clear gold
of late summer, of opening autumn,
the dawn eagle sunning himself on the highest tree,
the mountain revealing herself unclouded, her snow
tinted apricot as she looked west,
tolerant, in her steadfastness, of the restless sun
forever rising and setting.
                              Now I am given
a taste of the grey foretold by all and sundry,
a grey both heavy and chill. I've boasted I would not care,
I'm London-born. And I won't. I'll dig in,
into my days, having come here to live, not to visit.
Grey is the price
of neighboring with eagles, of knowing
a mountain's vast presence, seen or unseen.

Presence

Though the mountain's the same warm-tinted ivory
as the clouds (as if a red ground had been laid beneath
not quite translucent white) and though the clouds
disguise its shoulders, and rise tall to left and right,
and soften the pale summit with mist,
                                      yet one perceives
the massive presence, obdurate, unconcerned
among those filmy guardians.

Open Secret

Perhaps one day I shall let myself
approach the mountain—
hear the streams which must flow down it,
lie in a flowering meadow, even
touch my hand to the snow.
Perhaps not. I have no longing to do so.
I have visited other mountain heights.
This one is not, I think, to be known
by close scrutiny, by touch of foot or hand
or entire outstretched body; not by any
familiarity of behavior, any acquaintance
with its geology or the scarring roads
humans have carved in its flanks.
This mountain's power
lies in the open secret of its remote
apparition, silvery low-relief
coming and going moonlike at the horizon,
always loftier, lonelier, than I ever remember.

RICHARD HUGO (1923–1982) ✳   *Hugo was born in Seattle and grew up in an industrial suburb of the city. In 1943 he joined the Air Force and went to Italy, where he flew bomber missions. He studied with Roethke at the University of Washington. His move to Montana to teach in 1964 has been described as a turning point in Montana literature. He brought a working-class poetry of direct statement and formal sophistication, along with a keen eye and empathy for the hard luck of western living. His book on writing,* The Triggering Town, *continues to be influential.*[50]

Montana Ranch Abandoned

Cracks in eight log buildings, counting sheds
and outhouse, widen and a ghost peeks out.
Nothing, tree or mountain, weakens wind
coming for the throat. Even wind must work
when land gets old. The rotting wagon tongue
makes fun of girls who begged to go to town.
Broken brakerods dangle in the dirt.

Alternatives were madness or a calloused moon.
Wood they carved the plowblade from
turned stone as nameless gray. Indifferent flies
left dung intact. One boy had to leave
when horses pounded night, and miles away
a neighbor's daughter puked. Mother's cry
to dinner changed to caw in later years.

Maybe raiding bears or eelworms made them quit,
or daddy died, or when they planted wheat
dead Flatheads killed the plant. That stove
without a grate can't warm the ghost.
Tools would still be good if cleaned, but mortar
flakes and log walls sag. Even if you shored,
cars would still boom by beyond the fence, no glance
from drivers as you till the lunar dust.

Montana Ranch, 1872. PHOTO: JACKSON.

What Thou Lovest Well Remains American

You remember the name was Jensen. She seemed old
always alone inside, face pasted gray to the window,
and mail never came. Two blocks down, the Grubskis
went insane. George played rotten trombone
Easter when they flew the flag. Wild roses
remind you the roads were gravel and vacant lots
the rule. Poverty was real, wallet and spirit,
and each day slow as church. You remember the threadbare
church groups on the corner, howling their faith
at stars, and the violent Holy Rollers
renting that barn for their annual violent sing
and the barn burned down when you came back from war.
Knowing the people you knew then are dead,
you try to believe these roads paved are improved,
the neighbors, moved in while you were away, good-looking,
their dogs well fed. You still have need
to remember lots empty and fern.
Lawns well trimmed remind you of the train
your wife took one day forever, some far empty town,
the odd name you never recall. The time: 6:23.
The day: October 9. The year remains a blur.
You blame this neighborhood for your failure.
In some vague way, the Grubskis degraded you
beyond repair. And you know you must play again
and again Mrs. Jensen pale at her window, must hear
the foul music over the good slide of traffic.
You loved them well and they remain, still with nothing

Laying tracks in the Prescott and Eastern Railroad in Arizona Territory, 1998.

to do, no money and no will. Loved them, and the gray
that was their disease you carry for extra food
in case you're stranded in some odd empty town
and need hungry lovers for friends, and need feel
you are welcome in the secret club they have formed.

Brief History

Dust was too thick every summer. Every winter
at least one animal died, a good friend,
and we forgot the burial ritual after our Bible
washed away in the flood. We mumbled anything
that occurred to us over the grave. Finally
only our wives were left to hate, our children
who ran off to Detroit and never came back.
How we raged at change, the year the ground
went fallow, the time our wheat grew purple
and the government couldn't explain. Less fish
in the lake every year, grain prices falling
and falling through dark air, the suicide bird
who showed us the good way out. The century
turned without celebration. We tried to find fun
in the calendar, the strange new number, nineteen.
It was women held us together. They cautioned
us calm the day we shouted we knew
where millions in diamonds were buried
and ran at cattle swinging the ax.
We forget that now. We are planning hard
for the century ahead.

JOHN HAINES (1924–) ✳   *Born in Virginia, Haines studied art with Hans Hofmann before turning to writing. He homesteaded in Alaska for more than twenty years and is the author of several major collections of poetry; a collection of reviews and essays,* Living Off the Country; *and a memoir of his Alaskan experiences,* The Stars, the Snow, the Fire. *Among his many honors are a Western States Arts Federation Lifetime Achievement Award.*[51]

There Are No Such Trees in Alpine, California

I wanted a house
on the shore of Summer Lake,
where the cottonwoods burn
in a stillness beyond October,
their fires warming the Oregon farms.

There John Fremont and his men
rested when they came down late
from the winter plateau,
and mended in the waning sunlight.

Sprawled among frayed tents
and balky campfires, they told
of their fellowship in fever,
stories torn from buffalo tongues,
words of wind in a marrowbone;
how the scorched flower of the prairie
came to ash on a shore of salt.

Then silent and half asleep,
they gazed through green smoke

at the cottonwoods, spent leaves
caught fire and falling,
gathering more light and warmth
from the hearth of the sun,
climbing and burning again.

And there I too wanted to stay . . .
speak quietly to the trees,
tell in a notebook sewn from
their leaves my brief of passage:
long life without answering speech,
grief enforced in that absence;
much joy in the weather,
spilled blood on the snow.

With a few split boards,
a handful of straightened nails,
a rake and a broom;
my chair by the handmade window,
the stilled heart come home
through smoke and falling leaves.

   (1970)

The Eye in the Rock

A high rock face above Flathead Lake,
turned east where the light
breaks at morning over the mountain.

An eye was painted here by men
before we came, part of an Indian face,
part of an earth
scratched and stained by our hands.

It is only rock, blue or green,
cloudy with lichen,
changing in the waterlight.

Yet blood moves in this rock,
seeping from the fissures;
the eye turned inward, gazing back
into the shadowy grain,
as if the rock gave life.

And out of the fired mineral
come these burned survivors,
sticks of the wasting dream:

thin red elk and rusty deer,
a few humped bison,
ciphers and circles without name.

Not ice that fractures rock,
nor sunlight, nor the wind
gritty with sand has erased them.
They feed in their tall meadow,
cropping the lichen a thousand years.

Over the lake water comes this light
that has not changed,
the air we have always known . . .

They who believed that stone,
water and wind might be quickened
with a spirit like their own,
painted this eye that the rock might see.

(1975)

CAROLYN KIZER (1925–) ✳   *Born in Spokane, Washington, Kizer was educated at Sarah Lawrence College. In 1959 she founded* Poetry Northwest, *which she edited until 1965. Her book* Yin *won the 1985 Pulitzer Prize for poetry. In addition to numerous books of poems, she has published* Carrying Over: Translations from Chinese, Urdu, Macedonian, Hebrew, and French-African. *With formal elegance and biting sarcasm, Kizer's poems are a revolt against the sentimentality and piety of genteel verse.*[52]

from Running Away from Home

I
Most people from Idaho are crazed rednecks
Grown stunted in ugly shadows of brick spires,
Corrupted by fat priests in puberty,
High from the dry altitudes of Catholic towns.

Spooked by plaster madonnas, switched by sadistic nuns,
Given sex instruction by dirty old men in skirts,
Recoiling from flesh-colored calendars, bloody gods,
Still we run off at the mouth, we keep on running,

Like those rattling roadsters with vomit-stained back seats,
Used condoms tucked beneath floor-mats,
That careened down hairpin turns through the blinding rain
Just in time to hit early mass in Coeur d'Alene!

Dear Phil, Dear Jack, Dear Tom, Dear Jim,
Whose car had a detachable steering-wheel;
He'd hand it to his scared, protesting girl,
Saying, "Okay *you* drive"—steering with his knees;

Covered wagon encounters an automobile on the trail near Big Springs, Nebraska, 1912. PHOTO: A. L. WESTGARD.

Jim drove Daddy's Buick over the railroad tracks,
Piss-drunk, just ahead of the Great Northern freight
Barrelling its way thru the dawn, straight for Spokane.
O the great times in Wallace & Kellogg, the good clean fun!

Dear Sally, Dear Beth, Dear Patsy, Dear Eileen,
Pale, faceless girls, my best friends at thirteen,
Knelt on cold stone, with chillblained knees, to pray,
"Dear God, Dear Christ! Don't let him go All The Way!

O the black Cadillacs skidding around corners
With their freight of drunken Jesuit businessmen!
Beautiful daughters of lumber-kings avoided the giant
Nuptial Mass at St. Joseph's, and fled into nunneries.

The rest live at home; bad girls who survived abortions,
Used Protestant diaphragms, or refused the sacred obligation
Of the marriage bed, scolded by beat-off priests,
After five in five years, by Bill, or Dick, or Ted.

I know your secrets; you turn up drunk by 10 A.M.
At the Beauty Shoppe, kids sent breakfastless to school.
You knew that you were doomed by seventeen,
Why should your innocent daughters fare better than you?

Young, you live on in me; even the blessed dead:
Tom slammed into a fire hydrant on his Indian Chief
And died castrated; Jim, fool, fell 4 stories from the roof
Of his jock fraternity at Ag. & Tech.;

And the pure losers, cracked up in training planes
In Utah; or shot by a nervous rookie at Fort Lewis;
At least they cheated the white-coiffed ambulance chasers
And death-bed bedevillers, and died in war in peace.

Some people from Spokane are insane salesmen
Peddling encyclopedias from door to door,
Trying to earn enough to flee to the happy farm
Before they jump from the Bridge or murder Mom;

Or cut up their children with sanctified bread-knives
Screaming, "You are Isaac, and I am Abraham!"
But it's too late. They are the salutary failures
Who keep God from getting a swelled head.

Some shoot themselves in hotel rooms, after gazing
At chromos of the Scenic Highway through the Cascades
Via Northern Pacific, or the old Milwaukee & St. Paul:
Those trains that won't stop rattling in our skulls!

First they construct crude crosses out of Band-Aids
And stick them to the mirror; then rip pages
From the Gideon Bible, roll that giant final joint,
A roach from *Revelations*, as they lie dying.

Bang! It's all over. Race through Purgatory,
At last unencumbered by desperate manuscripts
In the salesman's sample-case, along with the dirty shirts.
After Spokane, what horrors lurk in Hell?

DAVID WAGONER (1926–) ✳ *Wagoner, originally a midwesterner, became a student of Roethke and taught for many years at the University of Washington. The author of more than a dozen books, he has written plays and novels in addition to poetry, and has served as editor for* Poetry Northwest. *His poems work to mythologize the wilderness as the place Americans go to learn spiritual lessons.*[53]

Lost

Stand still. The trees ahead and bushes beside you
Are not lost. Wherever you are is called Here,
And you must treat it as a powerful stranger,
Must ask permission to know it and be known.
The forest breathes. Listen. It answers,
I have made this place around you.
If you leave it, you may come back again, saying Here.
No two trees are the same to Raven.
No two branches are the same to Wren.
If what a tree or a bush does is lost on you,
You are surely lost. Stand still. The forest knows
Where you are. You must let it find you.

Breaking Camp

Having spent a hard-earned sleep, you must break camp in the mountains
At the break of day, pulling up stakes and packing,
Scattering your ashes,
And burying everything human you can't carry. Lifting
Your world now on your shoulders, you should turn
To look back once

At a place as welcoming to a later dead-tired stranger
As it was to your eyes only the other evening,
As the place you've never seen
But must hope for now at the end of a day's rough journey:
You must head for another campsite, maybe no nearer
Wherever you're going
Than where you've already been, but deeply, starkly appealing
Like a lost home: with water, the wind lying down
On a stretch of level earth,
And the makings of a fire to flicker against the night
Which you, travelling light, can't bring along
But must always search for.

Meeting a Bear

If you haven't made noise enough to warn him, singing, shouting,
Or thumping sticks against trees as you walk in the woods,
Giving him time to vanish
(As he wants to) quietly sideways through the nearest thicket,
You may wind up standing face to face with a bear.
Your near future,
Even your distant future, may depend on how he feels
Looking at you, on what he makes of you
And your upright posture
Which, in his world, like a down-swayed head and humped shoulders,
Is a standing offer to fight for territory
And a mate to go with it.
Gaping and staring directly are as risky as running:
To try for dominance or moral authority
Is an empty gesture,
And taking to your heels is an invitation to a dance

The U.S. Geological Expedition, led by Hayden, near Jackson, Wyoming Territory, 1871.

Which, from your point of view, will be no circus.
He won't enjoy your smell
Or anything else about you, including your ancestors
Or the shape of your snout. If the feeling's mutual,
It's still out of balance:
He doesn't *care* what you think or calculate; your disapproval
Leaves him as cold as the opinions of salmon.
He may feel free
To act out all his own displeasures with vengeance:
You would do well to try your meekest behavior,
Standing still
As long as you're not mauled or hugged, your eyes downcast.
But if you must make a stir, do everything sidelong,
Gently and naturally,
Vaguely oblique. Withdraw without turning and start saying
Softly, monotonously, whatever comes to mind
Without special pleading:
Nothing hurt or reproachful to appeal to his better feelings.
He has none, only a harder life than yours.
There is no use singing
National anthems or battle hymns or alma maters
Or any other charming or beastly music.
Use only the dullest,
Blandest, most colorless, undemonstrative speech you can think of,
Bears, for good reason, find it embarrassing
Or at least disarming
And will forget their claws and cover their eyeteeth as an answer.
Meanwhile, move off, yielding the forest floor
As carefully as your honor.

ALLEN GINSBERG (1926–   ) ✳ *When* Howl and Other Poems, *including "Sunflower Sutra," was published by City Lights Books in 1956, the book immediately became an American classic. Its publisher, Lawrence Ferlinghetti, was arrested on obscenity charges but later acquitted. Ginsberg remained central in the San Francisco literary scene of the Beats, though he has made his home in New York for many years.*[54]

Sunflower Sutra

I walked on the banks of the tincan banana dock and sat down under the huge
    shade of a Southern Pacific locomotive to look at the sunset over the box
    house hills and cry.
Jack Kerouac sat beside me on a busted rusty iron pole, companion, we thought
    the same thoughts of the soul, bleak and blue and sad-eyed, surrounded by
    the gnarled steel roots of trees of machinery.
The oily water on the river mirrored the red sky, sun sank on top of final
    Frisco peaks, no fish in that stream, no hermit in those mounts, just
    ourselves rheumy-eyed and hung-over like old bums on the riverbank, tired and wily.
Look at the Sunflower, he said, there was a dead gray shadow against the sky,
    big as a man, sitting dry on top of a pile of ancient sawdust—
—I rushed up enchanted—it was my first sunflower, memories of Blake—my
    visions—Harlem
and Hells of the Eastern rivers, bridges clanking Joes Greasy Sandwiches, dead
    baby carriages, black treadless tires forgotten and unretreaded, the poem
    of the riverbank, condoms & pots, steel knives, nothing stainless, only
    the dank muck and the razor-sharp artifacts passing into the past—
and the gray Sunflower poised against the sunset, crackly bleak and dusty with
    the smut and smog and smoke of olden locomotives in its eye—
corolla of bleary spikes pushed down and broken like a battered crown, seeds
    fallen out of its face, soon-to-be-toothless mouth of sunny air, sunrays
    obliterated on its hairy head like a dried wire spiderweb,
leaves stuck out like arms out of the stem, gestures from the sawdust root,
    broke pieces of plaster fallen out of the black twigs, a dead fly in its ear,

Unholy battered old thing you were, my sunflower O my soul, I loved you then!

The grime was no man's grime but death and human locomotives,

all that dress of dust, that veil of darkened railroad skin, that smog of
    cheek, that eyelid of black mis'ry, that sooty hand or phallus or
    protuberance of artificial worse-than-dirt—industrial—modern—all that
    civilization spotting your crazy golden crown—

and those blear thoughts of death and dusty loveless eyes and ends and
    withered roots below, in the home-pile of sand and sawdust, rubber dollar
    bills, skin of machinery, the guts and innards of the weeping coughing
    car, the empty lonely tincans with their rusty tongues alack, what more
    could I name, the smoked ashes of some cock cigar, the cunts of
    wheelbarrows and the milky breasts of cars, wornout asses out of chairs &
    sphincters of dynamos—all these

entangled in your mummied roots—and you there standing before me in the
    sunset, all your glory in your form!

A perfect beauty of a sunflower! a perfect excellent lovely sunflower
    existence! a sweet natural eye to the new hip moon, woke up alive and
    excited grasping in the sunset shadow sunrise golden monthly breeze!

How many flies buzzed round you innocent of your grime, while you cursed the
    heavens of the railroad and your flower soul?

Poor dead flower? when did you forget you were a flower? when did you look at
    your skin and decide you were an impotent dirty old locomotive? the ghost
    of a locomotive? the specter and shade of a once powerful mad American locomotive?

You were never no locomotive, Sunflower, you were a sunflower!

And you Locomotive, you are a locomotive, forget me not!

So I grabbed up the skeleton thick sunflower and stuck it at my side like a scepter,

and deliver my sermon to my soul, and Jack's soul too, and anyone who'll listen,

—We're not our skin of grime, we're not our dread bleak dusty imageless
    locomotive, we're all golden sunflowers inside, blessed by our own seed &
    hairy naked accomplishment-bodies growing into mad black formal sunflowers
    in the sunset, spied on by our eyes under the shadow of the mad locomotive
    riverbank sunset Frisco hilly tincan evening sitdown vision.

Berkeley, 1955

PHILIP LEVINE (1928–) ✳ *Levine was born and educated in Detroit. That place and his experiences in a*
succession of industrial jobs enter many of his poems, leading him to be regarded as a
poet of working-class life. The poems included here have a more domestic sense of
place. Levine lived in various parts of the country before settling in Fresno, California,
where he taught for many years before his recent retirement.[55]

Waking in March

Last night, again, I dreamed
my children were back at home,
small boys huddled in their separate beds,
and I went from one to the other
listening to their breathing—regular,
almost soundless—until a white light
hardened against the bedroom wall,
the light of Los Angeles burning south
of here, going at last as we
knew it would. I didn't waken.
Instead the four of us went out
into the front yard and the false dawn
that rose over the Tehachipis and stood
in our bare feet on the wet lawn
as the world shook like a burning house.
Each human voice reached us
without sound, a warm breath on the cheek,
a dry kiss.
          Why am I so quiet?
This is the end of the world, I am dreaming
the end of the world, and I go from bed
to bed bowing to the small damp heads

of my sons in a bedroom that turns
slowly from darkness to fire. Everyone
else is gone, their last words
reach us in the language of light.
The great eucalyptus trees along the road
swim in the new wind pouring
like water over the mountains. Each day
this is what we waken to, a water
like wind bearing the voices of the world,
the generations of the unborn chanting
in the language of fire. This will be
tomorrow. Why am I so quiet?

Snails

The leaves rusted in the late winds
of September, the ash trees bowed
to no one I could see. Finches
quarrelled among the orange groves.

I was about to say something final
that would capture the meaning
of autumn's arrival, something
suitable for bronzing,

something immediately recognizable
as so large a truth it's totally untrue,
when one small white cloud—not much
more than the merest fragment of mist—

passed between me and the pale
thin cuticle of the mid-day moon
come out to see the traffic and dust
of Central California. I kept quiet.

The wind stilled, and I could hear
the even steady ticking of the leaves,
the lawn's burned hay gasping
for breath, the pale soil rising

only to fall between earth and heaven,
if heaven's there. The world would escape
to become all it's never been
if only we would let it go

streaming toward a future without
purpose or voice. In shade the ground
darkens, and now the silver trails
stretch from leaf to chewed off leaf

of the runners of pumpkin to disappear
in the cover of sheaves and bowed grass.
On the fence blue trumpets of glory
almost closed—music to the moon,

laughter to us, they blared all day
though no one answered, no one
could score their sense or harmony
before they faded in the wind and sun.

ADRIENNE RICH (1929–   ) ✳ *Born in Baltimore and educated at Radcliffe College, Rich has lived in California since 1984. Early in her distinguished career she won acclaim for mastering traditional poetic forms. She later moved to free verse and expanded forms, but retained her thematic concern for the possibilities of personal and political transformation. She has published more than fifteen books of poetry and several highly regarded prose works, including* What Is Found There: Notebooks on Poetry and Politics.[56]

from An Atlas of the Difficult World

I

A dark woman, head bent, listening for something
—a woman's voice, a man's voice or
voice of the freeway, night after night, metal streaming downcoast
past eucalyptus, cypress, agribusiness empires
THE SALAD BOWL OF THE WORLD, gurr of small planes
dusting the strawberries, each berry picked by a hand
in close communion, strawberry blood on the wrist,
Malathion in the throat, communion,
the hospital at the edge of the fields,
prematures slipping from unsafe wombs,
the labor and delivery nurse on her break watching
planes dusting rows of pickers.
Elsewhere declarations are made: at the sink
rinsing strawberries flocked and gleaming, fresh from market
one says: "On the pond this evening is a light
finer than my mother's handkerchief
received from her mother, hemmed and initialled
by the nuns of Belgium."
One says: "I can lie for hours
reading and listening to music. But sleep comes hard.
I'd rather lie awake and read."   One writes:
"Mosquitoes pour through the cracks

in this cabin's walls, the road
in winter is often impassable,
I live here so I don't have to go out and act,
I'm trying to hold onto my life, it feels like nothing."
One says: "I never knew from one day to the next
where it was coming from: I had to make my life happen
from day to day.   Every day an emergency.
Now I have a house, a job from year to year.
What does that make me?"
In the writing workshop a young man's tears
wet the frugal beard he's grown to go with his poems
hoping they have redemption stored
in their lines, maybe will get him home free.   In the classroom
eight-year-old faces are grey.   The teacher knows which children
had not broken fast that day,
remembers the Black Panthers spooning cereal.

————————

I don't want to hear how he beat her after the earthquake,
tore up her writing, threw the kerosene
lantern into her face waiting
like an unbearable mirror of his own.   I don't
want to hear how she finally ran from the trailer
how he tore the keys from her hands, jumped into the truck
and backed it into her.   I don't want to think
how her guesses betrayed her—that he meant well, that she
was really the stronger and ought not to leave him
to his own apparent devastation.   I don't want to know
wreckage, dreck, and waste, but these are the materials
and so are the slow lift of the moon's belly
over wreckage, dreck, and waste, wild treefrogs calling in
another season, light and music still pouring over
our fissured, cracked terrain.

✳

Cliff House and Seal Rocks, San Francisco, California, 1902.   PHOTO: H. G. PEABODY.

———————

Within two miles of the Pacific rounding
this long bay, sheening the light for miles
inland, floating its fog through redwood rifts and over
strawberry and artichoke fields, its bottomless mind
returning always to the same rocks, the same cliffs, with
ever-changing words, always the same language
—this is where I live now.   If you had known me
once, you'd still know me now though in a different
light and life.   This is no place you ever knew me.
But it would not surprise you
to find me here, walking in fog, the sweep of the great ocean
eluding me, even the curve of the bay, because as always
I fix on the land.   I am stuck to earth.   What I love here
is old ranches, leaning seaward, lowroofed spreads between rocks
small canyons running through pitched hillsides
liveoaks twisted on steepness, the eucalyptus avenue leading
to the wrecked homestead, the fogwreathed heavy-chested cattle
on their blond hills.   I drive inland over roads
closed in wet weather, past shacks hunched in the canyons
roads that crawl down into darkness and wind into light
where trucks have crashed and riders of horses tangled
to death with lowstruck boughs.   These are not the roads
you knew me by.   But the woman driving, walking, watching
for life and death, is the same.

V
Catch if you can your country's moment, begin
where any calendar's ripped-off: Appomattox
Wounded Knee, Los Alamos, Selma, the last airlift from Saigon
the ex-Army nurse hitch-hiking from the debriefing center; medal
            of spit on the veteran's shoulder

—catch if you can this unbound land these states without a cause
earth of despoiled graves and grazing these embittered brooks
these pilgrim ants pouring out from the bronze eyes, ears,
          nostrils,
the mouth of Liberty
               over the chained bay waters
                             San Quentin:
once we lost our way and drove in under the searchlights to the
          gates
end of visiting hours, women piling into cars
the bleak glare aching over all
                       Where are we moored?   What
                       are the bindings?   What be-
                       hooves us?

Driving the San Francisco–Oakland Bay Bridge
no monument's in sight but fog
prowling Angel Island muffling Alcatraz
poems in Cantonese inscribed on fog
no icon lifts a lamp here
history's breath blotting the air
over Gold Mountain   a transfer
of patterns like the transfer of African appliqué
to rural Alabama   voices alive in legends, curses
tongue-lashings
               poems on a weary wall
And when light swivels off Angel Island and Alcatraz
when the bays leap into life
                    views of the Palace of Fine Arts,
                    TransAmerica
when sunset bathes the three bridges
                       still

old ghosts crouch hoarsely whispering
under Gold Mountain

—————

North and east of the romantic headlands there are roads into tule
          fog
places where life is cheap poor quick unmonumented
Rukeyser would have guessed it coming West for the opening
of the great red bridge   *There are roads to take* she wrote
when you think of your country   driving south
to West Virginia Gauley Bridge silicon mines the flakes of it
          heaped like snow, death-angel white
—poet journalist pioneer mother
uncovering her country: *there are roads to take*

GARY SNYDER (1930–) ✳   *Snyder's* Turtle Island *won the 1975 Pulitzer Prize for poetry. He has lived, traveled, and worked in California, the Pacific Northwest, and Japan. Currently teaching part-time at the University of California at Davis, he lives in the Sierra foothills of northern California, where he works on ecological issues through his local Yuba Watershed Institute.*[57]

Mid-August at Sourdough Mountain Lookout

Down valley a smoke haze
Three days heat, after five days rain
Pitch glows on the fir-cones
Across rocks and meadows
Swarms of new flies.

I cannot remember things I once read
A few friends, but they are in cities.
Drinking cold snow-water from a tin cup
Looking down for miles
Through high still air.

Piute Creek

One granite ridge
A tree, would be enough
Or even a rock, a small creek,
A bark shred in a pool.
Hill beyond hill, folded and twisted
Tough trees crammed
In thin stone fractures
A huge moon on it all, is too much.
The mind wanders. A million
Summers, night air still and the rocks
Warm. Sky over endless mountains.
All the junk that goes with being human
Drops away, hard rock wavers
Even the heavy present seems to fail
This bubble of a heart.
Words and books
Like a small creek off a high ledge
Gone in the dry air.

A clear, attentive mind
Has no meaning but that
Which sees is truly seen.
No one loves rock, yet we are here.

Night chills. A flick
In the moonlight
Slips into Juniper shadow:
Back there unseen
Cold proud eyes
Of Cougar or Coyote
Watch me rise and go.

I Went Into the Maverick Bar

I went into the Maverick Bar
In Farmington, New Mexico.
And drank double shots of bourbon
                    backed with beer.
My long hair was tucked under a cap
I'd left the earring in the car.

Two cowboys did horseplay
                by the pool tables,
A waitress asked us
                where are you from?
a country-and-western band began to play
"We don't smoke Marijuana in Muskokie"
And with the next song,
                a couple began to dance.

They held each other like in High School dances
                in the fifties;
I recalled when I worked in the woods
                and the bars of Madras, Oregon.
That short-haired joy and roughness—
                America—your stupidity.
I could almost love you again.

We left—onto the freeway shoulders—
                under the tough old stars—
In the shadow of bluffs
                I came back to myself,
To the real work, to
                "What is to be done."

JOSÉ MONTOYA (1932–) ✳   *Though he has published slightly, Montoya has written poems significant in the development of Chicano poetry, a literary movement linked, in its early years, with the farmworkers' movement. He founded the Royal Chicano Air Force (originally the Rebel Chicano Art Front) in Sacramento, a Mexican-American artists' cooperative. His poems make heavy use of caló, a barrio dialect combining Spanish and English.*[58]

from Faces at the First Farmworkers Constitutional Convention

Just the other day
In Fresno,
In a giant arena
Architectured

Family of chile pepper pickers.   PHOTO: © KEITH WOOD/TONY STONE

To reject the very poor,
César Chávez brought
The very poor
Together
In large numbers.

Cuatrocientos delegados
On the convention floor
Alone
And a few
Thousand more
In the galleries—

And outside
(. . . parecía el mercado de Toluca!)

The very poor had come
Together
For protection—

Thousands
From the chaos
Of past shameful harvests,
Culminating
That humble man's
Awesome task
Of organizing
The unorganizables!

Farmworkers!
(Workers of the fields!)

Campesinos!
(Peones de los campos de labores!)

Not lifeless executives.
Not, stranger yet,
Pompous politicians!

What I saw
Were the familiar
Faces
Of yester grapes
And labor camps.

Body dragging faces
Baked in the oven
Valle de Coachella
And frost-blistered
En las heladas de Sanger
During pruning time.

Faces that have
Dealt with
Exploiters and
Deporters
Y con contratistas
Chuecos.

Faces!

Faces black
From Florida with love
And Coca Cola

Y Raza
De Chicago
Brown Brown
y de Tejas
y Arabes de Lamont
y Filipinos de Delano
y así gente
That had come
From all the fields
Of all the farmlands
Of America

Farmworkers!
Campesinos!
The very poor!

The unorganizables—
Now, at a convention!

Yet,
No fancy vinyl-covered
Briefcases here,
No Samsonite luggage
Or Botany 500s,

Sólo ropa del trabajo
Pero bien planchadita
Y portafolios sencillos
De cartón
Y cada quien con su
Mochilita
Y taquitos
En el parking lot

Where old acquaintances
Renew friendships
And compare the
Different experiences
Of late

No longer merely
Comparing wages and
Camp conditions like
Before . . .

       (. . . ¿a cuánto andan pagando
       pa'ya pa'la costa?)

New queries now, reflecting
The different experiences
Of late . . .

       (and how many times were
       you arrested, brother?)

And the talk of the market
Place continues
And they listen to
Boastful, seasoned travelers
Who have left, for the time
Being, at least,
The well-worn routes
Of the harvest-followers
And they talk of
Strange sounding places . . .

(. . . pos sabe que yo andaba
en el boicoteo pa'ya pa'
filadelfia.)

The talk of the market place,
The parking place
The market lot
The parking lot
Where the families
Were bedded down
For three days
Amidst amistad
Y canciónes

Canciónes y más canciónes

Singing de colores,
About solidaridad
Pa'siempre
And we shall overcome
En Español

Singing, singing . . .

Even inside
On that floor of decorum
Singing
In defiance
Of Mr. Roberts' own rules!

Singing
Singing and joking

(... el que esté en acuerdo
con mi moción, que me la apele!)

Ca Ca car ca ja das
and table pounding
Belly rolls

Then
Earnestly, without embarrassment,
Back to work.
Faces!

Faces de farmworkers—
Organized!
Confident!
Unafraid!

Resoluteness
Without impudence—

(... me dispensa hermano director,
pero mi gente no ha comido.)

Faces!

Faces de campesinos,
Faces of the very poor
Confident,
Unafraid—

The unorganizables,
The people of the earth—

La gente de la tierra
Today
Very seriously
Contemplating
The ratification
Of Article 37
For history
And forever!

RICHARD SHELTON (1933–) ✳ *Born in Idaho, Shelton is the author of nine books of poetry and a memoir,*
Going Back to Bisbee. He has lived since 1956 in Southern Arizona, where he is
Regents Professor of English at the University of Arizona. Since 1974 he has
conducted writer's workshops in prisons; eight books of poetry and prose by men
in those workshops have been published.[59]

Sonora for Sale

this is the land of gods in exile
they are fragile and without pride
they require no worshipers

we come down a white road in the moonlight
dragging our feet like innocents
to find the guilty already arrived
and in possession of everything

we see the stars as they were years ago
but for us it is the future
they warn us too late

we are here we cannot turn back
soon we hold out our hands
full of money
this is the desert
it is all we have left to destroy

Because the Moon Comes

straight up from the mountain
rising to the surface of the sky
like the hidden possibility
of madness
escaped for everyone to see

and the wandering stars
who are said to rule our lives
wander on in darkness

I feel a need to lie down
among the stones
and caress any of them
who have survived

N. SCOTT MOMADAY (1934–) ✴

Kiowa poet, novelist, and painter Scott Momaday won the 1969 Pulitzer Prize for his novel House Made of Dawn. *He studied with Yvor Winters at Stanford University and is a professor of English at the University of Arizona. He was given the name Tsoai-talee, meaning "rock-tree-boy," to commemorate his having been taken as an infant to Devil's Tower, Wyoming, a sacred place in Kiowa tradition.*[60]

The Delight Song of Tsoai-talee

I am a feather on the bright sky
I am the blue horse that runs in the plain
I am the fish that rolls, shining, in the water
I am the shadow that follows a child
I am the evening light, the lustre of meadows
I am an eagle playing with the wind
I am a cluster of bright beads
I am the farthest star
I am the cold of the dawn
I am the roaring of the rain
I am the glitter on the crust of the snow
I am the long track of the moon in a lake
I am a flame of four colors
I am a deer standing away in the dusk
I am a field of sumac and the pomme blanche
I am an angle of geese in the winter sky
I am the hunger of a young wolf
I am the whole dream of these things

You see, I am alive, I am alive
I stand in good relation to the earth
I stand in good relation to the gods
I stand in good relation to all that is beautiful
I stand in good relation to the daughter of Tsen-tainte
You see, I am alive, I am alive

The Colors of Night

1. White

An old man's son was killed far away in the Staked Plains. When the old man heard of it he went there and gathered up the bones. Thereafter, wherever the old man ventured, he led a dark hunting horse which bore the bones of his son on its back. And the old man said to whomever he saw: "You see how it is that my son now consists in his bones, that his bones are polished and so gleam like glass in the light of the sun and moon, that he is very beautiful."

2. Yellow

There was a boy who drowned in the river, near the grove of thirty-two bois d'arc trees. The light of the moon lay like a path on the water, and a glitter of low brilliance shone in it. The boy looked at it and was enchanted. He began to sing a song that he had never heard before; only then, once, did he hear it in his heart, and it was borne like a cloud of down upon his voice. His voice entered into the bright track of the moon, and he followed after it. For a time he made his way along the path of the moon, singing. He paddled with his arms and legs and felt his body rocking down into the swirling water. His vision ran along the path of light and reached across the wide night and took hold of the moon. And across the river, where the path led into the shadows of the bank, a black dog emerged from the river, shivering and shaking the water from its hair. All night it stood in the waves of grass and howled the full moon down.

3. Brown

On the night before a flood, the terrapins move to high ground. How is it that they know? Once there was a boy who took up a terrapin in his hands and looked at it for a long time, as hard as he could look. He succeeded in memorizing the terrapin's face, but he failed to see how it was that the terrapin knew anything at all.

4. Red

There was a man who had got possession of a powerful medicine. And by means of this medicine he made a woman out of sumac leaves and lived with her for a time. Her eyes flashed, and her skin shone like pipestone. But the man abused her, and so his medicine failed. The woman was caught up in a whirlwind and blown apart. Then nothing was left of her but a thousand withered leaves scattered in the plain.

5. Green

A young girl awoke one night and looked out into the moonlit meadow. There appeared to be a tree; but it was only an appearance; there was a shape made of smoke; but it was only an appearance; there was a tree.

6. Blue

One night there appeared a child in the camp. No one had ever seen it before. It was not bad-looking, and it spoke a language that was pleasant to hear, though none could understand it. The wonderful thing was that the child was perfectly unafraid, as if it were at home among its own people. The child got on well enough, but the next morning it was gone, as suddenly as it had appeared. Everyone was troubled. But then it came to be understood that the child never was, and everyone felt better. "After all," said an old man, "how can we believe in the child? It gave us not one word of sense to hold on to. What we saw, if indeed we saw anything at all, must have been a dog from a neighboring camp, or a bear that wandered down from the high country."

7. Purple

There was a man who killed a buffalo bull to no purpose, only he wanted its blood on his hands. It was a great, old, noble beast, and it was a long time blowing its life away. On the edge of the night the people gathered themselves up in their grief and shame. Away in the west they could see the hump and spine of the huge beast which lay dying along the edge of the world. They could see its bright blood run into the sky, where it dried, darkening, and was at last flecked with flakes of light.

8. Black

There was a woman whose hair was long and heavy and black and beautiful. She drew it about her like a shawl and so divided herself from the world that not even Age could find her. Now and then she steals into the men's societies and fits her voice into their holiest songs. And always, just there, is a shadow which the firelight cannot cleave.

GEORGE KEITHLEY (1935–) ✳ *Keithley was born in Chico, California. His epic poem* The Donner Party *chronicles the 1846 journey of a group of families from Springfield, Illinois, who set out by wagon train for California. The group is remembered for their suffering and cannibalism when they became trapped in winter snow in the Sierras. Keithley retraced the party's route, using both fact and invention to tell their story. He has published several other books of poems, as well as scholarly work in* American Literature.[61]

from The Donner Party

from LAND LOGIC
We crept beneath our quilts at Pilot Peak.
I tossed all night, badgered by our bad luck.
I prayed we had seen the end of it. But no . . .

We woke to find the Peak was wrapped in snow!
Its dome wore a cap of fresh fallen snow.
Its flanks were wrinkled with crisp white creases.

I saw the dismay in many faces
and heard the fatigue in my friends' voices.
The advent of autumn was an unhappy omen . . .

We were weeks from California, and someone
must travel to Sutter's settlement
on the Sacramento river and ride back

with provisions. Flour and dried meat. On pack
horses or mules. "My wife's a sparrow,
she has no hips," I said, "she has no shadow."

Ladies laughed at this. I added, "And we know
our little ones are too weak to go on
eating like lizards." I spoke at midday

as the sun crossed over us and dried away
a fine-spun frost . . . Stanton and McCutchen
on plodding mounts set out for Sutter's place.

The sun scorched the sky and still a trace
of snow remained upon the peak. We kept
our cattle grazing by a running pool.

A week passed, the water every day was cool
and clean. On most mornings the sun seemed slow
to warm, the grass looked glossy with moisture.

We wanted only to rest, at this juncture.
Seeing the snow, no one wished to look back
on our bad luck or talk of it anymore.

Reflection only led us to deplore
the sudden end of summer and lament
the time we wasted in this trap. Whole days

spent unloading. Stupid disputes. Delays
caused by the cattle roaming or Hastings' wrong
advice . . . We were warned that to survive

we must lay up grass and water for a dry drive
of two days. Which meant at worst we might
travel a day and a night—where we instead

wandered a week in the desert and left dead
a third of our herd of cattle. Add a third
of the wagons abandoned, still it doesn't explain

all the destruction done. We could never regain
the time taken, or our goods and livestock left
on the salt. But this was not the only cost.

There is a land logic which we lost . . .
A sense of the likelihood of new terrain
to sustain us. The same logic that lives

in our blood, telling us that bottomland gives
promise for planting. Or for example,
the simple certainty that we would find

spring water among rocks when the sun reclined
on green slopes gleaming like good pasture.
But we hurried out only to discover

a prickly patch of greasewood growing over
the dry soil, white with alkali . . .
Nothing in nature was what it might seem!

The promise of finding forage by a stream
proved false as well—both banks were bare
although the current there cut swift and deep.

We lost the last advantage which could keep
our company from harm. It was this sense
of the land that had departed in a dream
while we went on like souls that are still asleep.

LUCILLE CLIFTON (1936–) ✳

Born in Depew, New York, Clifton was educated at the State University of New York at Fredonia and at Howard University. She taught for many years at the University of California at Santa Cruz. A distinguished writer of poetry, fiction, and children's books, she has won many awards including an Emmy Award from the American Academy of Television Arts and Sciences and the title of Poet Laureate of the State of Maryland, where she now lives.[62]

crazy horse names his daughter

sing the names of the women sing
the power full names of the women sing
White Buffalo Woman who brought the pipe
Black Buffalo Woman and Black Shawl
sing the names of the women sing
the power of name in the women sing
the name i have saved for my daughter sing
her name to the ties and baskets and
the red tailed hawk will take her name and
sing her power to WakanTanka sing
the name of my daughter sing she is
They Are Afraid Of Her.

crazy horse instructs the young men but in their grief they forget

cousins if i be betrayed
paint my body red and
plunge it in fresh water.
i will be restored. if not
my bones will turn to stone
my joints to flint and my spirit
will watch and wait.

it is more than one hundred years.
grandmother earth rolls her shoulders
in despair. her valleys are flooded
fresh with water and blood.
surely the heart of crazy horse must rise
and rebone itself.
to me my tribes.
to me my horses.
to me my medicine.

the message of crazy horse

i would sit in the center of the world,
the Black Hills hooped around me and
dream of my dancing horse. my wife

was Black Shawl who gave me the daughter
i called They Are Afraid Of Her.
i was afraid of nothing

except Black Buffalo Woman.
my love for her i wore
instead of feathers. i did not dance

i dreamed. i am dreaming now
across the worlds. my medicine is strong.
my medicine is strong in the Black basket
of these fingers. i come again through this

Black Buffalo Woman. hear me;
the hoop of the world is breaking.
fire burns in the four directions.
the dreamers are running away from the hills.
i have seen it. i am crazy horse.

LAWSON FUSAO INADA (1938–) ✳ *Inada was born a Sansei (third-generation Japanese American) in Fresno, California, and lives in Oregon. He lived during World War II with his family in "evacuation camps," then studied writing in Fresno, Berkeley, and Iowa. Also a bassist, his poetry has been strongly influenced by jazz. "My favorite form of 'publishing'—live," he writes, "in the bardic and jazz traditions."*[63]

From Our Album

I. "Before the War"
"Before the war"
means Fresno, a hedged-in house,
two dogs in the family.

Blackie, the small one, mine,
lapped at his insides
on the floorboard, on the way to the doctor.

Jimmy, my father's shepherd,
wouldn't eat after the evacuation.
He wouldn't live with another master

✳

Japanese evacuees arriving at Manzanar, California, a government internment center, spent the evening stuffing straw into sacks, these to serve as mattresses (1942).   PHOTO: AP/WIDE WORLD PHOTOS.

and pined away, skin and bone.

With feelings more than pride,
we call him our one-man dog.

II. Mud
Mud in the barracks—
a muddy room, a chamber pot.

Mud in the moats
around each barracks group.

Mud on the shoes
trudging to the mess hall.

Mud in the swamp
where the men chopped wood.

Mud on the guts
under a loaded wagon—

crushed in the mud by the wheel.

III. Desert Songs
1. All That We Gathered
Because there was little else to do,
they led us to the artillery range
for shells, all that we gathered,
and let us dig among dunes
for slugs, when they were through.

Because there was little else to do,
one of them chased a stray
with his tail between his legs
and shot him through the head.

2. Shells
A desert tortoise—
something mute and hard—

something to decorate
a desert Japanese garden:

gnarled wood, smooth
artillery shells for a border.

When a guard
smashes one, the shell

cracks open and the muscles ooze.

3. It Is Only Natural
The pheasant is an Oriental creature,
so it is only natural
that one should fly into camp

and, famished by rations and cans,
break out in secret, native dance
over a fire, on a black coal stove.

4. Song of the 442nd
Caged creatures
have curious moods.

Some of them choose
to be turned

loose in a group,
to take their chances

in the open.

5. Steers
Because a dentist
logically drives a butcher truck,

I rode with my father
to the slaughterhouse on an afternoon.

Not hammers, not bullets,
could make him close his eyes.

6. He Teaches
He jerks the eyes
from birds, feet
from lizards,

and punishes
ants with the gaze
of a glass.

And with his sly
gaze, his child's face,
he teaches

what has its place,
and must be
passed on to others.

IV. Song of Chicago
When the threat lessened,
when we became tame,
my father and friends
took a train to Chicago

for factory work,
for packaging bolts.
One grew a mustache
and called himself Carlos.

And they all made a home
with those of their own—

rats, bedbugs, blacks.

Concentration Constellation

In this earthly configuration,
we have, not points of light,
but prominent barbs of dark.

It's all right there on the map.
It's all right there in the mind.
Find it. If you care to look.

Begin between the Golden State's
highest and lowest elevations
and name that location

Manzanar. Rattlesnake a line
southward to the zone
of Arizona, to the home
of natives on the reservation,
and call those *Gila, Poston.*

Then just take your time
winding your way across
the Southwest expanse, the Lone
Star State of Texas, gathering
up a mess of blues as you
meander around the banks
of the humid Mississippi; yes,
just make yourself at home
in the swamps of Arkansas,
for this is *Rohwer* and *Jerome.*

By now, you weary of the way.
It's a big country, you say.
It's a big history, hardly
halfway though—with *Amache*
looming in the Colorado desert,
Heart Mountain high in wide
Wyoming, *Minidoka* on the moon
of Idaho, then down to Utah's
jewel of *Topaz* before finding
yourself at northern California's
frozen shore of *Tule Lake* . . .

Now regard what sort of shape
this constellation takes.
It sits there like a jagged scar,
massive, on the massive landscape.
It lies there like the rusted wire
of a twisted and remembered fence.

JAMES WELCH (1940–) ❋   *Born in Browning, Montana, of Blackfeet and Gros Ventre parents, Welch grew up on the
Blackfeet and Fort Belknap reservations. He studied writing with Richard Hugo at the
University of Montana. His father once leased forty acres belonging to the Earthboy
family, hence Welch's first collection of poems,* Riding the Earthboy 40. *He has
published poetry and widely acclaimed fiction.*[64]

Harlem, Montana: Just off the Reservation

We need no runners here. Booze is law
and all the Indians drink in the best tavern.
Money is free if you're poor enough.
Disgusted, busted whites are running
for office in this town. The constable,
a local farmer, plants the jail with wild
raven-haired stiffs who beg just one more drink.
One drunk, a former Methodist, becomes a saint
in the Indian church, bugs the plaster man
on the cross with snakes. If his knuckles broke,
he'd see those women wail the graves goodbye.

Goodbye, goodbye, Harlem on the rocks,
so bigoted, you forget the latest joke,
so lonely, you'd welcome a battalion of Turks
to rule your women. What you don't know,
what you will never know or want to learn—
Turks aren't white. Turks are olive, unwelcome
alive in any town. Turks would use
your one dingy park to declare a need for loot.
Turks say bring it, step quickly, lay down and dead.

Here we are when men were nice. This photo, hung
in the New England Hotel lobby, shows them nicer
than pie, agreeable to the warring bands of redskins
who demanded protection money for the price of food.
Now, only Hutterites out north are nice. We hate
them. They are tough and their crops are always good.
We accuse them of idiocy and believe their belief all wrong.

Harlem, your hotel is overnamed, your children
are raggedy-assed but you go on, survive
the bad food from the two cafes and peddle
your hate for the wild who bring you money.
When you die, if you die, will you remember
the three young bucks who shot the grocery up,
locked themselves in and cried for days, we're rich
help us, oh God, we're rich.

Christmas Comes to Moccasin Flat

Christmas comes like this: Wise men
unhurried, candles bought on credit (poor price
for calves), warriors face down in wine sleep.
Winds cheat to pull heat from smoke.

Friends sit in chinked cabins, stare out
plastic windows and wait for commodities.
Charlie Blackbird, twenty miles from church
and bar, stabs his fire with flint.

When drunks drain radiators for love
or need, chiefs eat snow and talk of change,
an urge to laugh pounding their ribs.
Elk play games in high country.

Medicine Woman, clay pipe and twist tobacco,
calls each blizzard by name and predicts
five o'clock by spitting at her television.
Children lean into her breath to beg a story:

Something about honor and passion,
warriors back with meat and song,
a peculiar evening star, quick vision of birth.
Blackbird feeds his fire. Outside, a quick 30 below.

JON ANDERSON (1940–   ) ✳   *Anderson has lived and taught in Tucson, Arizona, since the 1960s. His work, Dave Smith has written, has been influential in "establishing the style of contemporary poetry, that crystalline vulnerability." This elegy is set on the Rosebud reservation, where U.S. soldiers fought a battle on June 17, 1876, against the Cheyenne and Lakota Sioux under the leadership of Crazy Horse. A week later came the battle at the Little Bighorn.[66]*

Rosebud

There is a place in Montana where the grass stands up two feet,
Yellow grass, white grass, the wind
On it like locust wings & the same shine.
Facing what I think was south, I could see a broad valley
& river, miles into the valley, that looked black & then trees.
To the west was more prairie, darker
Than where we stood, because the clouds
Covered it; a long shadow, like the edge of rain, racing toward us.
We had been driving all day, & the day before through South Dakota
Along the Rosebud, where the Sioux
Are now farmers, & go to school, & look like everyone.
In the reservation town there was a Sioux museum
& 'trading post,' some implements inside: a longbow
Of shined wood that lay in its glass case, reflecting light.
The walls were covered with framed photographs,
The Oglala posed in fine dress in front of a few huts,
Some horses nearby: a feeling even in those photographs
The size of a book, of spaciousness.
I wanted to ask about a Sioux holy man, whose life
I had recently read, & whose vision had gone on hopelessly
Past its time: I believed then that only a great loss
Could make us feel small enough to begin again.

Sioux camp at Pine Ridge, South Dakota, 1890. PHOTO: G. E. TRAGER.

The woman behind the counter
Talked endlessly on; there was no difference I could see
Between us, so I never asked.
                              The place in Montana
Was the *Greasy Grass* where Custer & the Seventh Cavalry fell,
A last important victory for the tribes. We had been driving
All day, hypnotized, & when we got out to enter
The small, flat American tourist center we began to argue.
And later, walking between the dry grass & reading plaques,
My wife made an ironic comment: I believe it hurt the land, not
Intentionally; it was only meant to hold us apart.
Later I read of Benteen & Ross & those who escaped,
But what I felt then was final: lying down, face
Against the warm side of a horse, & feeling the lulls endlessly,
The silences just before death. The place might stand for death,
Every loss rejoined in a wide place;
Or it is rest, as it was after the long drive,
Nothing for miles but grass, a long valley to the south
& living in history. Or it is just a way of living
Gone, like our own, every moment.
Because what I have to do daily & what is done to me
Are a number of small indignities, I have to trust that
Many things we all say to each other are not intentional,
That every indirect word will accumulate
Over the earth, & now, when we may be approaching
Something final, it seems important not to hurt the land.

LORNA DEE CERVANTES (1940–) ✳

Cervantes grew up in San Jose, California. She was the founder of Mango Press, an important early publisher of Chicano writing. In her poems, the frontier, as the unknown terrain against which one's strength must be tested, has moved from the wilderness to the tense and risky streets of the urban West.[67]

Freeway 280

Las casitas near the gray cannery,
nestled amid wild abrazos of climbing roses
and man-high red geraniums
are gone now. The freeway conceals it
all beneath a raised scar.

But under the fake windsounds of the open lanes,
in the abandoned lots below, new grasses sprout,
wild mustard remembers, old gardens
come back stronger than they were,
trees have been left standing in their yards.
Albaricoqueros, cerezos, nogales . . .
Viejitas come here with paper bags to gather greens.
Espinaca, verdolagas, yerbabuena . . .

I scramble over the wire fence
that would have kept me out.
Once, I wanted out, wanted the rigid lanes
to take me to a place without sun,
without the smell of tomatoes burning
on swing shift in the greasy summer air.

Maybe it's here
en los campos extraños de esta ciudad
where I'll find it, that part of me
mown under
like a corpse
or a loose seed.

Colorado Blvd.

I wanted to die so I walked
the streets. Dead night,
black as iris, cold as the toes
on a barefoot drunk. Not a sound
but my shoes asking themselves over:
What season is this? Why is the wind
stuttering in its stall of nightmares?
Why courage or the bravery
of dripping steel? Given branches
rooted to their cunning, a kind
of snow lay fallow upon the hearth
of dried up trunks, wan and musing
like an absent guitarist strumming
wildly what she's forgotten most.
Bats fell about me like fire
or dead bark from my brow beaten
autumn. A kind of passing through
and when it called, the startled bird
of my birth, I left it, singing,
or fallen from its nest, it was silent
as the caves of my footfalls left
ridden in their absent burials.
What good was that? My cold
hearing, nothing, more desire
than protection. When would it come?
In that clove of cottonwood, perhaps
that shape in the mist, secret
as teeming lions? Is it my own
will that stalks me? Is it in
the slowed heart of my beatings

Los Angeles, at night, seen from Inspiration Point, Mount Lowe, 1950.

or the face that mists when
I least expect it? Frost covered
the windshields of the left
behind autos. In his parking
lot, my savior rests, semi-automatic
poised at my nipple or the ear
I expose to witches and thieves:
Here it is. Will you kill for it?

SIMON ORTIZ (1941–) ✳   *Ortiz is a native of Acoma Pueblo in New Mexico. In the fifties he read and was*
influenced by the Beat writers—Jack Kerouac, Allen Ginsberg, Gary Snyder, and others;
later he found common ground with Pablo Neruda, Nazim Hikmet, and other
international writers with a political sensibility. His poems also draw on the oral
tradition of his people.[65]

A Story of How a Wall Stands

At Aacqu, there is a wall
almost 400 years old
which supports hundreds
of tons of dirt and bones—
it's a graveyard built on a
steep incline—and it looks
like it's about to fall down
the incline but will not for
a long time.

My father, who works with stone,
says, "That's just the part you see,
the stones which seem to be
just packed in on the outside,"
and with his hands puts the stone and mud
in place. "Underneath what looks like loose stone,
there is stone woven together."
He ties one hand over the other,
fitting like the bones of his hands
and fingers. "That's what is
holding it together."

"It is built that carefully,"
he says, "the mud mixed
to a certain texture," patiently
"with the fingers," worked
in the palm of the hand. "So that
placed between the stones, they hold
together for a long, long time."

He tells me those things,
the story of them worked
with his fingers, in the palm
of his hands, working the stone
and the mud until they become
the wall that stands a long, long time.

Canyon de Chelly

Lie on your back on stone,
the stone carved to fit
the shape of yourself.
Who made it like this,
knowing that I would be along
in a million years and look
at the sky being blue forever?

My son is near me. He sits
and turns on his butt
and crawls over to stones,
picks one up and holds it,
and then puts it into his mouth.
The taste of stone.
What is it but stone,
the earth in your mouth.
You, son, are tasting forever.

We walk to the edge of the cliff
and look down into the canyon.
On this side, we cannot see
the bottom cliff edge but looking
further out, we see fields,
sand furrows, cottonwoods.
In winter, they are softly gray.
The cliffs' shadows are distant,
hundreds of feet below;
we cannot see our own shadows.
The wind moves softly into us.
My son laughs with the wind;
he gasps and laughs.

Canyon de Chelly. PHOTO: ANSEL ADAMS.

We find gray root, old wood,
so old, with curious twists
in it, curving back into curves,
juniper, piñon, or something
with hard, red berries in spring.
You taste them, and they are sweet
and bitter, the berries a delicacy
for bluejays. The plant rooted
fragilely into a sandy place
by a canyon wall, the sun bathing
shiny, pointed leaves.

My son touches the root carefully,
aware of its ancient quality.
He lays his soft, small fingers on it
and looks at me for information.
I tell him: wood, an old root,
and around it, the earth, ourselves.

ROBERT HASS (1941–) ✳ *California poet Robert Hass grew up in San Francisco and attended St. Mary's College*
and Stanford University. Influenced by the work of Chinese and Japanese poets, his three
volumes of poems bear the precision in detail and image of that work. Both lyric and
meditative, his poems of coastal California blend sensual engagement with moral
concern for how human acts shape the land.[68]

Palo Alto: The Marshes

For Mariana Richardson (1830–1891)

1
She dreamed along the beaches of this coast.
Here where the tide rides in to desolate
the sluggish margins of the bay,
sea grass sheens copper into distances.
Walking, I recite the hard
explosive names of birds:
egret, killdeer, bittern, tern.
Dull in the wind and early morning light,
the striped shadows of the cattails
twitch like nerves.

2
Mud, roots, old cartridges, and blood.
High overhead, the long silence of the geese.

3
"We take no prisoners," John Fremont said
and took California for President Polk.
That was the Bear Flag War.
She watched it from the Mission San Rafael,

named for the archangel (the terrible one)
who gently laid a fish across the eyes
of saintly, miserable Tobias
that he might see.
The eyes of fish. The land
shimmers fearfully.
No archangels here, no ghosts,
and terns rise like seafoam
from the breaking surf.

4
Kit Carson's antique .45, blue,
new as grease. The roar
flings up echoes,
row on row of shrieking avocets.
The blood of Francisco de Haro,
Ramón de Haro, José de los Reyes Berryessa
runs darkly to the old ooze.

5
The star thistles: erect, surprised,

6
and blooming
violet caterpillar hairs. One
of the de Haros was her lover,
the books don't say which.
They were twins.

7

In California in the early spring
there are pale yellow mornings
when the mist burns slowly into day.
The air stings
like autumn, clarifies
like pain.

8

Well I have dreamed this coast myself.
Dreamed Mariana, since her father owned the land
where I grew up. I saw her picture once:
a wraith encased in a high-necked black silk
dress so taut about the bones there were hardly ripples
for the light to play in. I knew her eyes
had watched the hills seep blue with lupine after rain,
seen the young peppers, heavy and intent,
first rosy drupes and then the acrid fruit,
the ache of spring. Black as her hair
the unreflecting venom of those eyes
is an aftermath I know, like these brackish,
russet pools a strange life feeds in
or the old fury of land grants, maps,
and deeds of trust. A furious dun-
colored mallard knows my kind
and skims across the edges of the marsh
where the dead bass surface
and their flaccid bellies bob.

9

A chill tightens the skin
around my bones. The other California

and its bitter absent ghosts
dance to a stillness in the air:
the Klamath tribe was routed and they disappeared.
Even the dust seemed stunned,
tools on the ground, fishnets.
Fires crackled, smouldering.
No movement but the slow turning
of the smoke, no sound but jays
shrill in the distance and flying further off.
The flicker of lizards, dragonflies.
And beyond the dry flag-woven lodges
a faint, persistent slapping.
Carson found ten wagonloads
of fresh-caught salmon, silver
in the sun. The flat eyes stared.
Gills sucked the thin annulling air.
They flopped and shivered,
ten wagonloads. Kit Carson
burned the village to the ground.
They rode some twenty miles that day
and still they saw the black smoke
smear the sky above the pines.

10

Here everything seems clear,
firmly etched against the pale
smoky sky: sedge, flag, owl's clover,
rotting wharves. A tanker lugs silver
bomb-shaped napalm tins toward
port at Redwood City. Again,
my eye performs
the lobotomy of description.

Again, almost with yearning,
I see the malice of her ancient eyes.
The mud flats hiss as the tide turns.
They say she died in Redwood City,
cursing "the goddamned Anglo-Yankee yoke."

I I

The otters are gone from the bay
and I have seen five horses
easy in the grassy marsh
beside three snowy egrets.

Bird cries and the unembittered sun,
wings and the white bodies of the birds,
it is morning. Citizens are rising
to murder in their moral dreams.

Spring Rain

Now the rain is falling, freshly, in the intervals between sunlight,

a Pacific squall started no one knows where, drawn east as the drifts of
warm air make a channel;

it moves its own way, like water or the mind,

and spills this rain passing over. The Sierras will catch it as last snow
flurries before summer, observed only by the wakened marmots at ten
thousand feet,

and we will come across it again as larkspur and penstemon sprouting
along a creek above Sonora Pass next August,

where the snowmelt will have trickled into Dead Man's Creek and the
creek spilled into the Stanislaus and the Stanislaus into the San Joaquin
and the San Joaquin into the slow salt marshes of the bay.

That's not the end of it: the gray jays of the mountains eat larkspur seeds,
which cannot propagate otherwise.

To simulate the process, you have to soak gathered seeds all night in the
acids of coffee

and then score them gently with a very sharp knife before you plant them
in the garden.

You might use what was left of the coffee we drank in Lisa's kitchen
visiting.

There were orange poppies on the table in a clear glass vase, stained
near the bottom to the color of sunrise;

the unstated theme was the blessedness of gathering and the blessing of
dispersal—

it made you glad for beauty like that, casual and intense, lasting as long
as the poppies last.

PAT MORA (1942–) ✳   *A distinguished Chicana author from the Texas-Mexico borderland, Mora is the author of*
three books of poetry, a collection of essays, children's books, and a new poetry manuscript
titled A Mexican Quartet: Talk Show Interviews with Coatlicue the Aztec Goddess, Malinche
the Maligned, The Virgin of Guadalupe, and La Llorona: The Wailer.[69]

La Migra*

I
Let's play *La Migra*
I'll be the Border Patrol.
You be the Mexican maid.
I get the badge and sunglasses.
You can hide and run,
but you can't get away
because I have a jeep.
I can take you wherever
I want, but don't ask
questions because
I don't speak Spanish.
I can touch you wherever
I want but don't complain
too much because I've got
boots and kick—if I have to,
and I have handcuffs,
Oh, and a gun.
Get ready, get set, run.

*term used along the border for Border Patrol agents

II

Let's play *La Migra*
You be the Border Patrol.
I'll be the Mexican woman.
Your jeep has a flat,
and you have been spotted
by the sun.
All you have is heavy: hat,
glasses, badge, shoes, gun.
I know this desert,
where to rest,
where to drink.
Oh, I am not alone.
You hear us singing
and laughing with the wind,
Agua dulce brota aquí,aquí, aquí＊＊,
but since you can't speak Spanish,
you do not understand.
Get ready.

＊＊sweet water gushes here, here, here

TESS GALLAGHER (1943–) ✳

Gallagher was born and raised in the logging country of northwestern Washington, where she continues to live. She studied with Theodore Roethke, and her books include Instructions to the Double, Under Stars, *and* Amplitude. *The land has always exacted a price from those who work it. Residents of the Northwest who have taken their livelihood out of the now depleted forests face a new challenge, as this novelistic poem conveys.*[70]

Woodcutting on Lost Mountain

for Leslie and for Morris

Our father is three months dead
from lung cancer and you light another Camel,
ease the chainsaw into the log. You
don't need habits to tell us
you're the one most like him.
Maybe the least loved
carries injury farther into tenderness
for having first to pass through
forgiveness. You
passed through. "I think he respected me
at the end," as if you'd waited a lifetime
to offer yourself that in my listening.

"Top of the mountain!" your daughter cries.
She's ten, taking swigs with us
from the beer can in the January sun. We see
other mountain tops and trees forever.
A mountain *could* get lost in all this, right
enough, even standing on it, thinking this
is where you are.

Stump farm, Washington, 1906. PHOTO: C. H. PARK.

"Remember the cabins we built when we were
kids? The folks logging Deer Park and
Black Diamond." My brother, Morris, nods,
pulls the nose of the saw into the air as a chunk
falls. "We built one good one. They
brought their lunches and sat with us
inside—Spam sandwiches on white bread,
bananas for dessert and Mountain Bars, white
on the inside, pure sugar on
the inside—the way they hurt your teeth."

Sawdust sprays across his knee, his face
closes in thought. "Those whippings." He
cuts the motor, wipes his forehead with an arm.
"They'd have him in jail today. I used to beg
and run circles. You got it worse because you
never cried. It's a wonder we didn't
run away." "Away to where?" I say. "There's no
away when you're a kid. Before you can get there
you're home."

"Once he took you fishing and left me
behind," my brother says.
"I drew pictures of you sinking
all over the chicken house. I gave you a head
but no arms. We
could go back today and there
they'd be, boats
sinking all down the walls."

His daughter is Leslie, named after our father.
Then I think—'She's a logger's daughter,
just like me'—and the thought pleases as if

the past had intended this present. "You
didn't know you were doing it," I tell him,
"but you figured how to stay
in our childhood." "I guess I did. There's
nothing I'd rather do," he says, "than cut wood.
Look at that—" he points to stacks of logs
high as a house he's thinned from the timber—
"they're going to burn them. Afraid
somebody might take a good tree
for firewood, so they'll burn half a forest.
Damn, that's the Forest Service for you. Me—
I work here, they'll have to stop me."

Leslie carries split wood to the tailgate
and I toss it into the truck. We make
a game of it, trying to stack as fast
as her father cuts. "She's a worker,"
Morris says. "Look at that girl go.
Sonofagun, I wouldn't trade four boys for her.
No sir." He picks up the maul, gives a yell
and whacks down through the center of a block
thick as a man. It falls neatly into
halves. "Look at that! Now *that's* good wood.
That's beautiful wood," he says, like he
made it himself.

I tell him how the cells of trees
are like the blood cells of people, how trees
are the oldest organisms on earth. Before
the English cut the trees off Ireland, the Irish
had three dozen woods for green. He's impressed,
mildly, has his own way of thinking about trees.

Tomorrow a log pile will collapse
on him and he will just get out alive.

"Remember the time Dad felled the tree on us
and Momma saved us, pushed us into a ditch? It's
a wonder we ever grew up."

"One of the horses they logged with, Dick
was his name, Old Dick. They gave him
to Oney Brown and Dick got into the house
while everyone was gone and broke
all the dishes. Dishes—what could they mean
to a horse? Still, I think he knew
what he was doing."

Oney's wife, Sarah, had fifteen kids. She's
the prettiest woman I'll ever see. Her son,
Lloyd, took me down to the railroad tracks
to show me the dead hounds. "We had too many
so they had to shoot some." The hounds were
skeletons by then, but they haven't moved
all these years from the memory
of that dark underneath of boughs.
I look at them, stretched on their sides, twin
arches of bones leaping with beetles and
crawlers into the bark-rich earth. Skipper
and Captain—Cappy for short. Their names
and what seemed incomprehensible—a betrayal
which meant those who had care of you
might, without warning, make an end of you
in some godforsaken, heartless place. Lloyd spat
like a father between the tracks, took
my hand and led me back to the others.

Twenty years settles on the boys
of my childhood. Some of them loggers.
"It's gone," they tell me. "The Boom Days
are gone. We thought
they'd never end, there were
that many trees. But it's finished,
or nearly. Nothing but stumps
and fireweed now."

"Alaska," Morris says, "that's where the trees
are," and I think of them, like some lost tribe
of wanderers, their spires and bloodless blood
climbing cathedral-high into the moss-light
of days on all the lost mountains of
our childhoods.

Coming into the town we see the blue smoke
of the trees streaming like a mystery
the houses hold in common.
"Doesn't seem possible—," he says, "a tree
nothing but a haze you could
put your hand through."

"What'll you do next, after the trees are gone?"

"Pack dudes in for elk."

"Then what?"

"Die, I guess. Hell, I don't know, ask
a shoemaker, ask a salmon . . .
Remember that time I was hunting and got lost,

"Her daily duty": Cow and boys in front of schoolhouse, Okanogan, Washington, 1907. PHOTO: FRANK MATSURA.

forgot about the dark and me with no coat, no
compass? You and Dad fired rifles from the road
until I stumbled out. It
was midnight. But I got out. It's a wonder
I could tell an echo from a shot, I was so cold,
so lost. Stop cussing, I told the old man, I'm
home, ain't I? 'You're grown,' he kept saying,
'you're a grown man.'
I must be part wild. I must be part tree or part
deer. I got on the track and I was lost
but it didn't matter. I had to go where it led.
I must be part bobcat."

Leslie is curled under my arm, asleep.

"Truck rocks them to sleep," Morris says.
"Reminds me, I don't have a license for this
piece of junk. I hope I don't get stopped. Look
at her sleep! right in the middle of the day.
Watch this: 'Wake up honey, we're lost. Help me
get home. You went to sleep and got us lost.'
She must be part butterfly, just look at those eyes.
There—she's gone again. I'll have to carry
her into the house. Happens every time.
Watch her, we'll go up the steps and she'll be
wide awake the minute I open the door.
Hard to believe, we had to be carried into houses
once, you and me. It's a wonder we ever
grew up."

Tomorrow a log pile will collapse
and he'll just get out alive.

He opens the door. Her eyes start,
suddenly awake.

"See, what'd I tell you. Wide awake. Butterfly,
you nearly got us lost, sleeping so long.
Here, walk for yourself. We're home."

DAVID LEE (1944–) ✳   *David Lee lives in southern Utah and teaches at Southern Utah State College in Cedar City.*
His poems employ regional vernacular ranging from biblical diction to the banter of rural
ranch life. He is best known for his narrative poems about pig-farming published in
The Porcine Canticles.[71]

Behold

And came forth like Venus from an ocean of
heat waves, morning in his pockets and the buckets in his hands
he emerged from the grey shed, tobacco and wind
pursed together in song from his tight lips he gathered day
and went out to cast wheat before swine. And in
his mind he sang songs and thought thoughts, images of clay
and heat, wind and sweat, dreams of silver and
visions of green earth twisting the cups of his mind
he crossed his fence of wire, the south Utah steppes
bending the air into corners of sky he entered
the yard to feed his swine. And his pigs, they come.

Racehogs

John calls and sez Dave
when I say hello and I say hello John
and he sez come down Dave
you gotta see what I got
I say fine I'll be right there and he sez
bring Jan I'll show her too
and I said I will
so Jan and I got in the car to see
what John bought.

John bought four hogs
starved half to death, bones out
everywhere, snouts sharp enough
to root pine trees and the longest damn legs
I've seen. What do you think? he sez
and I don't say anything so he sez
I sez what do you think? and I say
them's pretty good-looking racehogs John
and he sez what? and I tell him
I heard about a place in Japan or California
(because he's never been there) where they
have a track and race hogs
on Tuesday nights and he sez do they
pay much? and I say yes or so I heard
maybe a hundred to win and he sez
goddam and I say those hogs
ought to be good with them long legs
and skinny bodies and he sez goddam.

Jan's walked off so I go find her
but she's mad and says I ought not to do that
and I say oh I was just bullshitting
but when we come back John's standing
by the fence throwing little pieces of feed
all around the pen making the hogs
hurry from one place to the next
and when I get up close he's smiling
and I can hear him whisper
while he throws the feed
run you skinny fuckers, run.

W. S. DI PIERO (1945–) ✳   *Originally from South Philadelphia, Di Piero lives in California and teaches at Stanford University. He is the author of six books of poems and two books of essays, as well as translations of works by Giacomo Leopardi, Sandro Penna, and Leonardo Sinisgalli. His poems of the West hold together in intricate tension the sacred and profane, history and the contemporary moment.*[72]

San Antonio de Padua

The soldier, the only one in sight,
stroked his skeletal, teenage moustache
and waved me through the gate.
A red-cross helicopter on its pad,
open-eyed and dense, like a housefly;
rows of tanks, half-tracks, other green vehicles;
rows of barracks with packs of new sports cars
squared off on sunny lots; basketball and tennis courts.

Adobe church, Alamo National Forest, New Mexico National Forest, 1908.   PHOTO: A. M. NEAL.

Road signs point to code-named spots
folded into the hills. In the Valley of the Oaks,
the first to answer Father Serra's mission bell
brought others. More came. Soon ten thousand sheep
grazed valley-wide around this hub of vineyards,
workshops, tannery, the church and plaza.
Hot wind running in the irrigation ditches
brings smells of sage and live oak. By the Church door,
an olive tree stands taller than the facade.
Wind turns its leaves. Dried grasses stir.
A red convertible squirts down the road,
its engine whine soaked up by the wind.

I came half-hoping to find something left
from that collaboration on divinity,
the Roman God planted in our sun.
Despite the sentry's word, I stopped a half-mile short
at an unmarked Mission Style building off the road.
The Mexican cleaningwoman, the only person there,
said it was, or used to be, the officers' club
(I saw a kitchenette stacked with whiskey cartons),
the rooms modelled after friars' cells,
but the real mission is down the road.
"Where is everybody?" "Oh," she said. "They're all here."
In the garden, I name what I remember.
Agave, wisteria, yucca, persimmon and fig,
"cactus" for the dozen kinds I count,
when a voice behind me says it's always water.
An old padre in coolie hat and smock
points to open trenches cut crosswise,
like the Church floorplan, up and down the garden.
"New pipes, but what good when there's no rain
for five years? We always need more water."

The cross blazed on a treetrunk two centuries ago
now lies exposed, complete, grown over in the oak flesh.
A pomegranate tree, the only plant from mission days,
bears small, waxy, Baby Jesus fruit. Outside,
I trace my map to crumbling beehive ovens,
then the massive irrigation system slaves dug.
The helicopter passes. Church walls drenched in ochre,
collapsed kilns for firing tiles, tens of thousands of tiles—
fire and dirt seem to enclose, include, everything.
I know an abstract painter who, to justify his work,
says that before our early ones painted shapes
of deer, bison, hands and spears,
they painted their own bodies, as if to pull earth over us
to protect us from heaven, or to prepare us
to make images of this world. Pink wash
aureoled around the windows, turquoise window frames,
red arches painted over arches, stencilled oak leaves . . .
Inside the cool church, above the altar,
old pudgy misshapen stars
tumble across the blue wood firmament.

Ice Plant in Bloom

From where I stood at the field's immaculate edge,
walking past the open patch of land that's money bounded,
in California's flat sunlight, by suburban shadows of houses
occupied by professors, lawyers, radically affluent do-gooders,
simple casual types, plus a few plumbers, children of lettuce-pickers
and microchip princes, grandchildren of goatherds and orchard keepers
who pruned and picked apricot trees that covered what wasn't yet
block after block. Vaporized by money, by the lords and ladies of money,

in one month, on one block, three bungalows bulldozed, and the tanky smells
of goatherds and, before them, dirt farmers who never got enough water,
held momentary in the air like an album snapshot's aura,
souls of roller-rink sweethearts and sausage-makers fleeing
heaps of crusty lath, lead pipe, tiny window casements,
then new foundations poured for cozy twelve-room houses.
So what was she doing in that field among weeds and ice plant?
The yellow and pink blooms spiking around her feet like glory?
Cranking her elbow as surveyors do, to a bored watcher in the distance,
she fanned the air, clouds running low and fast behind her.

A voice seeped through the moodless sunlight
as she seemed to talk to the flowers and high weeds.
She noticed me, pointed in my direction. Accusation, election,
I could not tell, nor if it was at me myself
or the green undeveloped space she occupied,
welded into her grid by traffic noise. *Okay!*
A word for me? A go-ahead? *Okay!* Smeared by the wind
and maybe not her own voice after all. I held my place.
She would be one of the clenched ministers adrift
in bus terminals and K-Marts, carrying guns
in other parts of America, except she dressed like a casual lady of money,
running shoes, snowbird sunglasses, wristwatch like a black birthday cake.
The voice, thin and pipey, came from the boy or girl,
blond like her, who edged into view as I tracked the shot. The child,
staring down while he cried his song, slowly tread the labyrinth
of ice plant's juicy starburst flesh of leaves.
Okay! He follows the nested space between flowers that bristle at his feet,
his or hers, while the desiccated California sky so far from heaven and hell
beams down on us beings of flower, water, and flesh before they turn to money.
The sky kept sliding through the tips of weeds. The sky left us behind.

ADRIAN C. LOUIS (1946–) ✳

An enrolled member of the Lovelock Paiute tribe, Louis was born and raised in Nevada. He has edited several tribal newspapers and teaches at Oglala Lakota College on the Pine Ridge Reservation of South Dakota. His poems give hard-edged testimony to Indian life today.[73]

Indian College Blues

Friday's all-staff meeting dissolves
into structure because time is money
and the *wasicu* neo-colonials in charge
have learned to ignore "Indian time."
The breed guest speaker is dressed
in black like a skinny witch Johnny Cash.
Self-proclaimed as an Indian expert
she launches into her talk about the ancient
Indian astronomy inherent
in a tribal history she herself has conjured
according to fullbloods sitting near me.
They ignore her and talk about the rodeo
or who got shot at and missed by his old lady
then wrecked his car like he was in a movie
after eluding the tribal cops
by speeding through a herd
of a thousand whiteface steers.
The cops threw him to the ground, cuffed him,
and then rubbed his face in fresh bullshit
only because the cops were his cousins.

The strange skinny woman lulls my mind away
from overhearing the story of the chase
because part of me pities her
and her bat-winged words whisk me away
with a brief, daft vision of Copernican Sioux.
Distracted momentarily, my ears
wander back to the renegade car crasher.
In the image of his cousins rubbing his face
into fresh cowshit I know he saw stars
and in his sight I see ancient campfires
twinkling in our ancestors'
earthly imitation of the night sky.

Somehow the witchy speaker does not know
the lessons of her own blood.
Her own people cannot see her
and her own people cannot hear her
but I am transported by the cowshit grace
of our Indian race
until the meeting so mercifully ends.

    for Robert Gay

LINDA HOGAN (1947–) ✳ *A Chickasaw writer living in Colorado, Hogan writes spare and elemental poems that draw on Indian heritage and on her profound understanding of the power of image and myth to convey the complexity of history. She has also published a novel titled* Mean Spirit.[74]

Bear Fat

When the old man rubbed my back
with bear fat
I dreamed the winter horses
had eaten the bark off trees
and the tails of one another.

I slept a hole into my own hunger
that once ate lard and bread
from a skillet seasoned with salt.

Fat was the light
I saw through
the eyes of the bear
three bony dogs leading men
into the grass-lined cave of sleep
to kill hunger
as it slept itself thin.

They grew fat
with the swallowed grease.

They ate even the wood-ashes
after the fire died
and when they slept,
did they remember back
to when they were wolves?

I am afraid of the future
as if I am the bear
turned in the stomach
of needy men
or the wolf become a dog
that will turn against itself
remembering what wildness was
before the crack of a gun,
before the men tried to kill it
or tame it
or tried to make it love them.

Map

This is the world
so vast and lonely
without end, with mountains
named for men
who brought hunger
from other lands,
and fear
of the thick, dark forest of trees
that held each other up,
knowing fire dreamed of swallowing them
and spoke an older tongue,

and the tongue of the nation of wolves
was the wind around them.
Even ice was not silent.
It cried its broken self
back to warmth.
But they called it
ice, wolf, forest of sticks,
as if words would make it something
they could hold in gloved hands,
open, plot a way
and follow.

This is the map of the forsaken world.
This is the world without end
where forests have been cut away from their trees.
These are the lines wolf could not pass over.
This is what I know from science:
that a grain of dust dwells at the center
of every flake of snow,
that ice can have its way with land,
that wolves live inside a circle
of their own beginning.
This is what I know from blood:
the first language is not our own.

There are names each thing has for itself,
and beneath us the other order already moves.
It is burning.
It is dreaming.
It is waking up.

AI (1947–) ✳ *Ai's father was Japanese, and her mother was of African-American, Choctaw Indian, Irish, and German descent. She lives in Arizona. Known for her dramatic monologues, she speaks here in the voice of J. Robert Oppenheimer, student of Eastern religion and leader of the Manhattan Project in Los Alamos, New Mexico, where the atomic bomb was invented.*[75]

The Testimony of J. Robert Oppenheimer

A Fiction

When I attained enlightenment,
I threw off the night like an old skin.
My eyes filled with light
and I fell to the ground.
I lay in Los Alamos,
while at the same time,
I fell
toward Hiroshima,
faster and faster,
till the earth,
till the morning
slipped away beneath me.
Some say when I hit
there was an explosion,
a searing wind that swept the dead before it,
but there was only silence,
only the soothing baby-blue morning
rocking me in its cradle of cumulus cloud,
only rest.

❋

The first nuclear explosion, July 16, 1945, New Mexico. The blast left a half-mile-wide crater.

PHOTO: AP/WIDE WORLD PHOTOS.

There beyond the blur of mortality,
the roots of the trees of Life and Death,
the trees William Blake called Art and Science,
joined in a kind of Gordian knot
even Alexander couldn't cut.

To me, the ideological high wire
is for fools to balance on with their illusions.
It is better to leap into the void.
Isn't that what we all want anyway?—
to eliminate all pretense
till like the oppressed who in the end
identifies with the oppressor,
we accept the worst in ourselves
and are set free.

In high school, they told me
all scientists
start from the hypothesis "what if"
and it's true.
What we as a brotherhood lack in imagination
we make up for with curiosity.
I was always motivated
by a ferocious need to know.
Can you tell me, gentlemen,
that you don't want it too?—
the public collapse,
the big fall smooth as honey down a throat.
Anything that gets you closer
to what you are.

Oh, to be born again and again
from that dark, metal womb,
the sweet, intoxicating smell of decay
the imminent dead give off
rising to embrace me.

But I could say anything, couldn't I?
Like a bed we make and unmake at whim,
the truth is always changing,
always shaped by the latest
collective urge to destroy.
So I sit here,
gnawed down by the teeth
of my nightmares.
My soul, a wound that will not heal.
All I know is that urge,
the pure, sibylline intensity of it.
Now, here at parade's end
all that matters:
our military readiness,
our private citizens
in a constant frenzy of patriotism
and jingoistic pride,
our enemies endless,
our need to defend infinite.
Good soldiers,
we do not regret or mourn,
but pick up the guns of our fallen.
Like characters in the funny papers,
under the heading
"Further Adventures of the Lost Tribe,"
we march past the third eye of History,

as it rocks back and forth
in its hammock of stars.
We strip away the tattered fabric
of the universe
to the juicy, dark meat,
the nothing beyond time.
We tear ourselves down atom by atom,
till electron and positron,
we become our own transcendent annihilation.

GREG PAPE (1947–   ) ✳   *A native of California, Pape was educated there and in Arizona. He lives and teaches in Montana and has published six books. His carefully seen poems about the western land and its ancient cultures are not so much elegies as a process of finding spiritual common ground with lives that have gone before.*[76]

Indian Ruins Along Rio de Flag

I'm learning how to read the rocks,
how to tell the difference between
those that lie where the magma
cooled and hardened, and those
that are the ruined walls of homes.

They lived here because of the river.
They sang the river where the sun shone,
where the night sky glittered.
I can almost hear them sometimes
when I cross the river.

Now it's a pitiful stream
lined with red and white signs
that read contaminated—an open
sewer we call Rio de Flag.
No one knows what they called it.

No one knows what they sang
when they saw the river of fire.
When the fire cooled and the dead
were sung they planted corn and squash
in the cinders and bathed their children

in the river and built their homes
of rocks that once were fire.

I'm learning how to watch the birds
as they fly off into the distance
until they turn into distance,
into nothing I can see, like spirits,
and then go on watching, as they must have,

until something in the distance
turns into birds again.

Making a Great Space Small

The sun is going down. A few miles
to the east on Navajo land the sheep scatter
and the people spit in the dust when the bombers
fly low making a great space small.
Last night snow filled the crevices

and the inner basin of the peaks. Frost
blackened the stems and leaves and broke
the necks of the marigolds. Now the wind
has died down. The sky is a dusty blue
streaked with contrails—the fear of a nation
at work in the sky. Down here curled seed heads
of grama grass are lighting up like candles
in the late sun, as they've done since before
there were Octobers. Now a flicker hammers
a juniper in the distance and the pinyons
glisten with voices of small birds. I feel
a fall sun on my face and hands, a breath
of ice at my neck.

      We say the sun is going down
and know it's not true. The truth is
we're turning away. If I know anything,
I know this: this is my body—ice, wind,
this light mending the grass, birdsong,
the spit in the dust, this argument that goes on.

JUAN FELIPE HERRERA (1948–) ✳ *Herrera has been active as a poet, editor, teatrista, and teacher since the mid-sixties. He teaches in the Chicano and Latin American Studies program at California State University in Fresno. His poems moved the political sensibility of early Chicano poetry toward a more surreal and scatlike technique.*[77]

Mission Street Manifesto

for all varrios

Blow out the jiving smoke the plastik mix the huddling straw of the dying mind
and rise sisters rise brothers and spill the song and sing the blood that calls
the heart the flesh that has the eyes and gnaws the chains and blow
and break through the fuse the military spell the dreams of foam
make the riff jump the jazz ignite the wheel burn the blade churn rise
and rise sisters rise brothers and spill the song and sing the blood that calls
the ancient drums the mineral fists the rattling bones of gold
on fire the lava flow the infinite stream the razor wave
through the helmet the holy gun the Junta the seething boot
shake it do the shing-a-ling the funky dog of sun and moon
pull out the diamonds from your soul the grip of light the stare of stars
rip the wires invade the air and twist the scales and tear the night
go whirling go singeing go shining go rumbling go rhyming
our handsome jaws of tender truth our shoulders of sweating keys
to crack the locks the vaults of hands the dome of tabernacle lies
and rise sisters rise brothers and spill the song and sing the blood that calls
out swing out the breathing drums the tumbling flutes the hungry strings
and spin a flash deep into the sorrow of the silent skull
the vanquished lips the conquered song the knot in the belly of earth
break out through the fenders the angel dust kiss the methadone rooms
go chanting libre chanting libre go chanting libre go

libre *La Mission* libre *El Salvador* libre *La Mujer*
the will of the worker now the destiny of children libre
blow out the jiving smoke the plastic mix the huddling straw of the dying mind
the patrolling gods the corporate saints the plutonium clouds
strike the right the new Right to crucify the right to decay
the triple K the burning cross the territorial rape game
and stop the neutron man the nuclear dream the assassination line
the alienation master the well groomed empire the death suit
and rise and rise libre libre and rise and rise and rise libre
and rise sisters rise brothers and spill the song and sing the blood that calls
blow out the jiving smoke the plastik mix the huddling straw of the dying mind
forever
forever
forever.

JOHN DANIEL (1948–) ✳   *Raised in the suburbs of Washington, D.C., Daniel has lived in the West since 1966,
working as a logger, railroad inspector, rock-climbing instructor, hod carrier, and writing
teacher. He has been a Wallace Stegner Fellow at Stanford University and now lives in
the Pacific Northwest, and he has published two books of poems and a collection of
essays on nature titled* The Trail Home.[78]

To Mt. St. Helens

You were the perfect one,
the saint of symmetry.
We glanced at your benign
bright face, and you shined back

Mount St. Helens, Washington, April 10, 1980. PHOTO: AP/WIDE WORLD PHOTOS.

your blessing, you smiled
peacefully upon us.
We didn't much believe
your smoke and stir, we thought
your restiveness would pass—
and then you shuddered hard
and blasted yourself across
four states, engulfed a lake,
gorged rivers with gray mud,
flattened entire forests
and whatever lives they held
in your searing smother.
Your evenness and grace
exploded twelve miles high,
then showered down as grit
on our trim lawns and gardens—
and there you slouch, smudged
and gaping, spewing smoke,
resting in your rubble.
You did it, Mt. St. Helens.
As all of us looked on
you stormed in solitude,
you shrugged and shook aside
what we called beautiful
as if none of us were here,
no animals, no trees,
no life at all outside
your ancient fiery joy—
I admired you, mountain,
but I never loved you until now.

Moment

for W. S. Di Piero

Squares of tended grass, roses
trimmed and mulched with chips, all
the blank front doors along
these gridded streets, neighborhood
I walk and carry docilely
in walks of mind—until
one yellow leaf shoots by
and I'm on edge again, I'm
walking fast through gusting air
that strips the maples, scattering
leaves and paper scraps
like some rousing consciousness
unbound by human blocks—as if
the wild god had wakened me,
or waked in me, not the clerk
who accounts for fallen birds,
the one we kicked upstairs,
but the god still ranging
in this world, that scatters us
to its unspoken need, and only
finds its way as we find ours.

LYNN EMANUEL (1949–) ✳ *Emanuel's richly textured poems track her memory back to childhood and growing up poor in Ely, Nevada. Many western writers have addressed, as does Emanuel, the use of western land for nuclear weapons testing; "The Planet Krypton" is one of the best, capturing the complexity and strangeness of that period and recalling the hope engendered at the dawning of the nuclear age.*[79]

What Ely Was

The mauve, the ocher of canned tamales, the dark silt
of gravy burning, the hominy's white knuckles;
fats that made a surface gleam like a pigeon's neck,
like a spill of gasoline, melt-down crusts of oleo
on the tuna casserole, toast that was blackened
to a piece of macadam, a singed field, a roof shingle.
The cool unguent of jam upon a spoon, but every sweet
thing has a sting. It was good for you, this needle, this pin.
Under the beautiful blue glass dome of plum preserves
was the bite of penicillin. I longed for chocolate both
sweet and bitter, fried green plantain, mustard, onion,
red tomato, rice and black beans in a pot, Moroccan olives
with cayenne, Haut-Brion, cabbage, ham. Somewhere
some green coast exported all I wanted of all I wanted,
a kingdom where my hunger fit, both mind and body, all of it.

The Planet Krypton

Outside the window the McGill smelter
sent a red dust down on the smoking yards of copper,
on the railroad tracks' frayed ends disappearing
into the congestion of the afternoon. Ely lay dull

and scuffed: a miner's boot toe worn away and dim,
while my mother knelt before the Philco to coax
the detonation from the static. From the Las Vegas
Tonapah Artillery and Gunnery Range the sound

of the atom bomb came biting like a swarm
of bees. We sat in the hot Nevada dark, delighted,
when the switch was tripped and the bomb hoisted
up its silky, hooded, glittering, uncoiling length;

it hissed and spit, it sizzled like a poker in a toddy.
The bomb was no mind and all body; it sent a fire
of static down the spine. In the dark it glowed like the coils
of an electric stove. It stripped every leaf from every

branch until a willow by a creek was a bouquet
of switches resinous, naked, flexible, and fine.
Bathed in the light of KDWN, Las Vegas,
my crouched mother looked radioactive, swampy,

glaucous, like something from the Planet Krypton.
In the suave, brilliant wattage of the bomb, we were
not poor. In the atom's fizz and pop we heard possibility
uncorked. Taffeta wraps whispered on davenports.

A new planet bloomed above us; in its light
the stumps of cut pine gleamed like dinner plates.
The world was beginning all over again, fresh and hot;
we could have anything we wanted.

JAMES GALVIN (1951–) ✳ *Raised in northern Colorado, Galvin is the author of four books of poetry and a beautiful and inventive prose book, **The Meadow**, that depicts the hundred-year history of a meadow and its neighboring inhabitants on the Colorado-Wyoming border. Clay and Frank, who appear in this poem, are characters in that book as well.*[80]

Western Civilization

for William Kittredge

I.
That woman still lives at her ranch.
You can ask her. Maybe
She knows. As near and far

As the rest of us can tell
The barn and sheds were built
In the Great Depression. Someone

Had money and a big idea.
Far and away the biggest
Idea I've ever seen.

Pat says there must've been
A hundred men, shepherds
And shearers, working there.

It's one of those things
That not only is, but seems,
Larger inside than out.

Potato farming, with irrigation pipeline.   PHOTO: © MARTIN ROGERS/TONY STONE

Like a planetarium or an orange,
Even with Wyoming around it,
And real stars flying away.

Just stick your head in there;
Its dark will make you dizzy.
It has an underneath

Too low to stand in unless
You are a sheep. The loft
Vaults like a dusky church.

2.
All that summer
I balanced water,

Coaxing the desert
Into pasture,

With eight cubic feet
Per second for two

Thousand acres.
Horseback, shovel

On my shoulder along
Miles of ditches:

Stalling here,
Releasing there,

Water over
The deepening green,

Keeping it living:
Herons and cranes

Regal in meadows,
Strings of ducklings

Frothing the ditch
To get away.

3.
One day riding ditches I saw Clay.
He was on the hill against the sky,
Flapping his arms at me.
They were going to bulldoze the corrals at the shearing sheds,

Intricate maze of gates and pens
Clay, as a kid, had built with his father,
Before they lost their ranch, before Frank died,
Before the family had to move away.

The new owner was razing everything.
I guess he had some kind of idea.
Clay didn't need any gates, but, as Pat said,
That's Clay.
I met them at the shearing sheds.
Pat held a wrecking bar like a steel snake.
I just can't stand tearin' apart all them guys's dreams,
He said, looking shy.
Hell is when you know where you are.

4.
On the barn roof a loose piece of tin
Flaps in the wind like a broken wing.
Wyoming whirls in the sun.

Up in the loft a pair of shears,
Oh, fifty or sixty years forgotten there,

Floats in noonlight, bearing up some dust,
Just a pair of spring-steel scissors,
Two knives joined at the hip, with smiling edges.

An owl the color of things left alone
Flaps out of the gable door.

Hell is when you know where you are:
Mazes of pens and gates dreaming sheep;
Miles of ditches dreaming green.

5.
No one living knows
Who built the shearing sheds,
Unless maybe that woman,
And I'm not about to ask her,
Ever since she tried
To stab her husband with a pair of scissors.
He was ninety-one
And barely held her off.
Later she claimed she was just
Trying to cut his heart
Medication out of his shirt
Pocket—dope, she called it—
And the old man had to leave
The ranch, where he didn't last long.

They bulldozed the corrals.
We got forty gates.
We took them someplace safe.

6.
Now the vast, dim barn floats like an ocean liner
Whose doldrums are meadows spinning into brush,
And everywhere you look Wyoming hurries off.

All night the stars make their escape.
In the loft a pair of shears cuts woolly moonlight.
All day a piece of roofing slaps in the wind.

A startled owl flaps out of the gable.
Hell is when you know where you are and it's beautiful.
You saved the gates for nothing.

You balanced the water to keep the green from spinning
Away into sage, the same gray as the wing
That just now shaded your eyes.

PAUL ZARZYSKI (1951–) ✳

Zarzyski grew up in Wisconsin and moved to Missoula to study poetry with Richard Hugo. When he was twenty-six years old he took up bronc-riding and competing on the rodeo circuit. He is one of the few poets who can claim a following both at cowboy poet gatherings and among literary readers.[81]

Trespasses

The penance for killing mountain goat is pain
and more pain. Knees swelling
like cumulus, I climbed beyond
all gravity, beyond quasar, the last
frontier of cosmos black
turning instantly
to quartz, a crystalline
hoarfrost ignited by light
stronger than sun—climbed to the land
where goats glide inaudibly
rock to rock, each step sheer
miracle. Angels are the sole form
of wisdom with innocence. Without halo,
without wing, goats gambol
black-horned through perpetual whiteness
they know safe from fall,
from all evil but this one
breathless aim and squeeze
it takes to splatter heaven
the color red. In this echo of guts end-
over-end, intestines flail with trachea
from stomach, from lungs—bagpipes

skirling punched and pummeled
to an avalanche of dream. The devil's
wet reflection glares up at me
from the hollow-ground
blade slicing hide and flesh
from the bone and soul I left behind.

Silos

against Augusta, Montana: prairie dovetailed
with Rockies, raptor with hard wind, hard
grass and grain, with cattle and antelope
with Flat Creek—rainbow
brown and brook trout—with buckbrush
coulee—jackrabbit and mule deer—
with snowberry, cocklebur and rosehip scrub
—Hungarian partridge and sharptail—
with sun and moon with Tabletop
and Steamboat Mountain, with Haystack
Butte, Gobblers' Knob, Bean Lake, and yardlight
to yardlight, that distant dark we love
between stars. Silos against Augusta:
honeybee with Hutterite with family ranch—
the Minuteman launching pads
against everything from Dearborn River
to jackfence to cowhorse and combine
rolling with the camber and cant, rolling
with the land. Ballistic Missile vaults
square off in a chain all their own
against the horizontal grain
of glacier and age: warheads

from Augusta, from earth still festering
cavalry repeating carbines
to the surface—shrapnel
through old scars—where cattle stir,
moon to salt lick to moon,
this veteran wind
once bulletproof, this distance
no longer dark, no longer living
out of sight and range.

JOY HARJO (1951–) ✳   *Born in Tulsa, Oklahoma, Harjo is an enrolled member of the Muscogee Tribe. She performs her poetry and plays saxophone with her band, Poetic Justice, and teaches at the University of New Mexico. She is one of the country's foremost Native American writers, combining elements of storytelling, prayer, traditional song, and jazz.[82]*

Sonata for the Invisible

for my son

We are comfortable on the rich grass stolen from arid beauty, and watch the sun beat on an ensemble of singers and dancers from a horse people from the north who aren't used to the heat.

They illustrate different dances to the crowd, who were fooled into thinking there's nothing left, but songs are a cue as to what walks among us unseen.

Ancestors stand with jackrabbit and saguaro—all of us beneath the flight of dipping hawks.

The drum makes a wedge into consciousness before the flute player begins melodic flight on notes based on a scale that has nothing to do with the construction of a piano in Europe.

This scale involves the relationship of the traveler's horse to the morning star and what the arc makes as it lovingly re-creates red dawn.

Somewhere far from here it is raining as steady as the pattern the grass makes and it has been raining hard for years.

The hawk makes an elegant scribble in the wind of mist and within this story is the flute player who acquires the secret of flying.

I hear the opening of the Bear Dance I saw performed at the Holiday Inn in Reno. Suddenly bears converged in that conference room as slot machines rang up pitiful gains and losses.

We joined the bear world as they danced for us, the same as we join the dancers spiraling from this lawn.

We have always been together.

Perhaps the World Ends Here

The world begins at a kitchen table. No matter what, we must eat to live.

The gifts of earth are brought and prepared, set on the table. So it has been since creation, and it will go on.

We chase chickens or dogs away from it. Babies teethe at the corners. They scrape their knees under it.

It is here that children are given instructions on what it means to be human. We make men at it, we make women.

At this table we gossip, recall enemies and the ghosts of lovers.

Our dreams drink coffee with us as they put their arms around our children. They laugh with us at our poor falling-down selves and as we put ourselves back together once again at the table.

This table has been a house in the rain, an umbrella in the sun.

Wars have begun and ended at this table. It is a place to hide in the shadow of terror. A place to celebrate the terrible victory.

We have given birth on this table, and have prepared our parents for burial here.

At this table we sing with joy, with sorrow. We pray of suffering and remorse. We give thanks.

Perhaps the world will end at the kitchen table, while we are laughing and crying, eating of the last sweet bite.

JIMMY SANTIAGO BACA (1952–) ✳ *New Mexican poet Jimmy Baca was born into a poor and troubled Chicano family and for some time was raised in an orphanage. At age ten he ran away and lived in the barrios of New Mexico. During a period of imprisonment he learned to read and write, finding his way back to the stories of his Indian and Hispanic elders. This awakening to ethnic identity led Baca to his redemptive work as a poet.*[83]

Invasions

for Eddie

6:00 A.M.
I awake and leave to fish
the Jemez.
Coronado rode
through this light, dark

green brush,
horse foaming saliva,
tongue red and dry
as the red cliffs.
Back then the air
was bright and crisp
with Esteban's death
at the hands of Zuni warriors.
Buffalo God, as he was called,
was dead, dead, dead,
beat the drums
and rattled gourds.
The skin of the Moor
was black
as a buffalo's nose,
hair kinky
as buffalo shag-mane.
No seven cities
of Cíbola gold were found.
Horses waded the Jemez,
white frothing currents
banking horse bellies,
beading foot armor,
dripping from sword scabbards.
I wade in
up to my thighs
in jeans,
throw hooked
salmon egg bait
out in shadowy shallows
beneath overhanging cottonwood, and
realize

I am the end result
of Conquistadores,
Black Moors,
American Indians,
and Europeans,
bloods rainbowing
and scintillating
in me
like the trout's flurrying
flank scales
shimmering a fight
as I reel in.
With trout
on my stringer
I walk downstream
toward my truck.
"How'd you do?" I ask
an old man walking past,
              "Caught four—biting pretty good
              down near that elm."
I walk south
like Jemez and Pecos pueblos
during 1690 uprisings,
when Spanish came north
to avenge their dead.
Indians fled
canyon rock shelters,
settling in present day
open plains.
Trout flails like a saber
dangling from scabbard stringer
tied to my belt,

chop-whacking long-haired weeds.
Peace here now. Bones
dissolved, weapons rusted.
I stop, check my sneaker prints
in moist sandy bank.
Good deep marks.
I clamber up an incline,
crouch in bushes
as my ancestors did,
peer at vacation houses
built on rock shelves,
sun decks and travel trailers—
the new invasion.

GARY SOTO (1954–) ✳ *Soto, the first Chicano poet to win mainstream literary recognition and honors, was raised in Fresno, California. He has published numerous books of poetry and recently has been working on books for children. This early poem, spare and metaphoric, powerfully evokes the relationship between the farmworker and the land in the San Joaquin Valley of Central California.*[84]

The Elements of San Joaquin

FIELD

The wind sprays pale dirt into my mouth
The small, almost invisible scars
On my hands.

The pores in my throat and elbows
Have taken in a seed of dirt of their own.

After a day in the grape fields near Rolinda
A fine silt, washed by sweat,
Has settled into the lines
On my wrists and palms.

Already I am becoming the valley,
A soil that sprouts nothing
For any of us.

WIND
A dry wind over the valley
Peeled mountains, grain by grain,
To small slopes, loose dirt
Where red ants tunnel.

The wind strokes
The skulls and spines of cattle
To white dust, to nothing,

Covers the spiked tracks of beetles,
Of tumbleweed, of sparrows
That pecked the ground for insects.

Evenings, when I am in the yard weeding,
The wind picks up the breath of my armpits
Like dust, swirls it
Miles away

And drops it
On the ear of a rabid dog,
And I take on another life.

WIND
When you got up this morning the sun
Blazed an hour in the sky,

A lizard hid
Under the curled leaves of manzanita
And winked its dark lids.

Later, the sky grayed,
And the cold wind you breathed
Was moving under your skin and already far
From the small hives of your lungs.

STARS
At dusk the first stars appear.
Not one eager finger points toward them.
A little later the stars spread with the night
And an orange moon rises
To lead them, like a shepherd, toward dawn.

SUN
In June the sun is a bonnet of light
Coming up,
Little by little,
From behind a skyline of pine.

The pastures sway with fiddle-neck
Tassels of foxtail.

At Piedra
A couple fish on the river's edge,
Their shadows deep against the water.
Above, in the stubbled slopes,
Cows climb down
As the heat rises
In a mist of blond locusts,
Returning to the valley.

RAIN
When autumn rains flatten sycamore leaves,
The tiny volcanos of dirt
Ants raised around their holes,
I should be out of work.

My silverware and stack of plates will go unused
Like the old, my two good slacks
Will smother under a growth of lint
And smell of the old dust
That rises
When the closet door opens or closes.

The skin of my belly will tighten like a belt
And there will be no reason for pockets.

FOG
If you go to your window
You will notice a fog drifting in.

The sun is no stronger than a flashlight.
Not all the sweaters
Hung in closets all summer

Could soak up this mist. The fog:
A mouth nibbling everything to its origin,
Pomegranate trees, stolen bicycles,

The string of lights at a used-car lot,
A Pontiac with scorched valves.

In Fresno the fog is passing
The young thief prying a window screen,
Graying my hair that falls
And goes unfound, my fingerprints
Slowly growing a fur of dust—

One hundred years from now
There should be no reason to believe
I lived.

DAYBREAK
In this moment when the light starts up
In the east and rubs
The horizon until it catches fire,

We enter the fields to hoe,
Row after row, among the small flags of onion,
Waving off the dragonflies
That ladder the air.

And tears the onions raise
Do not begin in your eyes but in ours,
In the salt blown
From one blister into another;

They begin in knowing
You will never waken to bear
The hour timed to a heart beat,
The wind pressing us closer to the ground.

When the season ends,
And the onions are unplugged from their sleep,
We won't forget what you failed to see,
And nothing will heal
Under the rain's broken fingers.

OFELIA ZEPEDA (1954–) ✳   *A member of the Tohono O'odham (formerly Papago) tribe, Zepeda was born and grew up in Stanfield, Arizona, a rural cotton-farming community. She authored the first grammar of the Tohono O'odham language, and writes poetry in both O'odham and English. She teaches linguistics and American Indian Studies at the University of Arizona.*[85]

People on Wayward Journeys

(Russian Thistle, Russian Tumbleweed)

They have no use for traffic lights
or crosswalks.
They take fate into their own hands
and roll across streets
in Chandler, Mesa, Coolidge,
and other cotton-field-infested towns.

Many become traffic statistics
under the wheels of Ford pickup trucks.
Luckier ones become temporary hood ornaments
and additions to car grills.

They make trails across the desert,
to the reservation,
they know no boundaries.
They journey from village to village
as if going for visits over coffee.
On Saturday afternoons
they roll early into the village dance,
semi-invited guests.

At night,
the meeting place is along horse corrals.
There most meet their destiny.

A few lucky ones will have winds
to set them free.
To continue their wayward journeys.
Origins unknown.
Destinations unclear.

Kitchen Sink

The light from the kitchen-door window comes through in a special way.
I can see the seasons change in my kitchen sink.
The movement of the sun is shadowed in that sink.
During the afternoon the sink is full with sunlight.
Not necessarily a good time to be washing dishes.

Later in the summer there is a sense of urgency as the shadow gets longer and begins to slant
as the sunlight starts to edge out of the sink.
I pretend the sunlight is going down the drain.
The light cannot be stopped by the plug in the drain.
It seeps down around the inner seal where water cannot go,
becoming a part of the darkness that is always a part of drains and pipes.
Winter is coming.
The air is probably cooler already.
I know this because of my sink.

BENJAMIN ALIRE SÁENZ (1954–) ✳   *Sáenz grew up in the desert of southern New Mexico. He writes fiction and essays in addition to poetry and teaches in the bilingual creative writing program at the University of Texas at El Paso. His work centers on coming to terms with the history of violence that has shaped both the West and his family.*[86]

Resurrections

California
Lent, 1990

The stones themselves will sing.

Broken, Incan roads. The stones laid perfect
on mountains of snow so stubborn
not even blazing suns could beat it into water.
But the Incans could tame such mountains. With a fire
of their own, they knew how to melt that ice.
Stone by stone, step by step, the ancients

walked the highest paths of earth. Stones,
tight knots that tied the world together. Roads, higher—
now stones are buried deep like bones
of Incan lords. I walked there barefoot
on cold stones. Those roads were perfect once again
until I woke. Those roads, like Incan hands
who built them, refuse to lie still
in the ground. They loosen the wasted land.

✳

My mother lost him young, her older brother. She gave
my brother his name "because the moment he was born
his name rose to my lips." Ricardo, "A friend
took a stone, and broke his skull wide open—
and broke my mother's heart." She walks with him
on a path they took to school. There, in the sun, he laughs
until she wakes. Been forty years,
and grief is glued to her. Anger rises
in her voice. "But *here*," she grabs his picture,
Here he is perfect. *Here* he is not broken."

✳

The beer I drink is good tonight,
almost sweet, but cold. The dead are close.
Calm, I sit, touch the photographs of those
I walked with. Grandparents, uncles, not one
generation was spared. A brother. A niece.
In the country of their final exile
their legs will not cross the border.
Their feet will not touch my earth again
but tonight I hear their steps. I swallow,

must finish the beer I have started. *Take this
all of you and drink. This is my blood.* Tired,
I drink from the cup, take the cold, within me now,
and wrap myself in faces of the dead:
stones which form a path where I walk still.

✳

The Mimbres buried their dead beneath their homes.
At night, softly, the buried
rose, re-entered the rooms of the living
as blankets woven with the heavy threads of memory,
blankets on which the Mimbres rested,
on which they slept, and dreamed.

MARILYN CHIN (1955–) ✳   *Poet and translator, Marilyn Chin was born in Hong Kong and raised in Portland,
Oregon. The author of two books of poems,* Dwarf Bamboo *and* The Phoenix Gone, the
Terrace Empty, *she now lives in California and teaches at San Diego State University.*[87]

How I Got That Name

an essay on assimilation

I am Marilyn Mei Ling Chin.
Oh, how I love the resoluteness
of that first person singular
followed by that stalwart indicative

of "be," without the uncertain i-n-g
of "becoming." Of course,
the name had been changed
somewhere between Angel Island and the sea,
when my father the paperson
in the late 1950s
obsessed with a bombshell blonde
transliterated "Mei Ling" to "Marilyn."
And nobody dared question
his initial impulse—for we all know
lust drove men to greatness,
not goodness, not decency.
And there I was, a wayward pink baby,
named after some tragic
white woman swollen with gin and Nembutal.
My mother couldn't pronounce the "r."
She dubbed me "Numba one female offshoot"
for brevity: henceforth, she will live and die
in sublime ignorance, flanked
by loving children and the "kitchen deity."
While my father dithers,
a tomcat in Hong Kong trash—
a gambler, a petty thug,
who bought a chain of chopsuey joints
in Piss River, Oregon,
with bootlegged Gucci cash.
Nobody dared question his integrity given
his nice, devout daughters
and his bright, industrious sons.
As if filial piety were the standard
by which all earthly men were measured.

Oh, how trustworthy our daughters,
how thrifty our sons!
How we've managed to fool the experts
in education, statistics and demography—
We're not very creative but not adverse to rote-learning.
Indeed, they can *use* us.
But the "Model Minority" is a tease.
We know you are watching now,
so we refuse to give you any!
Oh, bamboo shoots, bamboo shoots!
The further west we go, we'll hit east;
the deeper down we dig, we'll find China.
History has turned its stomach
on a black polluted beach—
where life doesn't hinge
on that red, red wheelbarrow,
but whether or not our new lover
in the final episode of "Santa Barbara"
will lean over a scented candle
and call us a "bitch."
Oh God, where have we gone wrong?
We have no inner resources!

Then, one redolent spring morning
the Great Patriarch Chin
peered down from his kiosk in heaven
and saw that his descendants were ugly.
One had a squarish head and a nose without a bridge.
Another's profile—long and knobbed as a gourd.
A third, the sad, brutish one
may never, never marry.

And I, his least favorite—
"not quite boiled, not quite cooked,"
a plump pomfret simmering in my juices—
too listless to fight for my people's destiny.
"To kill without resistance is not slaughter"
says the proverb. So, I wait for imminent death.
The fact that this death is also metaphorical
is testament to my lethargy.

So here lies Marilyn Mei Ling Chin,
married once, twice to so-and-so, a Lee and a Wong,
granddaughter of Jack "the patriarch" Chin
and the brooding Suilin Fong,
daughter of the virtuous Yuet Kuen Wong
and G. G. Chin the infamous,
sister of a dozen, cousin of a million,
survived by everybody and forgotten by all.
She was neither black nor white,
neither cherished nor vanquished,
just another squatter in her own bamboo grove
minding her poetry—
when one day heaven was unmerciful,
and a chasm opened where she then stood.
Like the jowls of a mighty white whale,
or the jaws of a metaphysical Godzilla,
it swallowed her whole.
She did not flinch nor writhe,
nor fret about the afterlife,
but stayed! Solid as wood, happily
a little gnawed, tattered, mesmerized
by all that was lavished upon her
and all that was taken away!

CAMPBELL MCGRATH (1962–) ✳

McGrath has traveled extensively in the United States and abroad. He has lived among the Umbandistas of Brazil and the Cargo Cultists of Vanuatu. He writes in the expansive tradition of Whitman. His poems of the American West make visionary new connections between place and history. They are poems in search of a renewed faith in the communal dream of democracy.[88]

Wheatfield Under Clouded Sky

Suppose Gauguin had never seen Tahiti. Suppose the *bêche-de-mer* and
    sandalwood trade had not materialized
and the Polynesian gods held fast in the fruit of Nuku Hiva and the milk-
    and-honey waters of Eiao.
Suppose that Europe during whichever century of its rise toward science
    had not lost faith in the soul.
Suppose the need for conquest had turned inward, as a hunger after
    clarity, a siege of the hidden fortress.
Suppose Gauguin had come instead to America. Suppose he left New
    York and traveled west by train
to the silver fields around Carson City where the water-shaped, salt- and
    heart-colored rocks
appeased the painter's sensibility and the ghost-veined filaments called
    his banker's soul to roost.
Suppose he died there, in the collapse of his hand-tunneled mine shaft,
    buried beneath the rubble of desire.
Suppose we take Van Gogh as our model. Suppose we imagine him alone
    in the Dakotas,
subsisting on bulbs and tubers, sketching wildflowers and the sod huts of
    immigrants as he wanders,
an itinerant prairie mystic, like Johnny Appleseed. Suppose what
    consumes him is nothing so obvious as crows

or starlight, steeples, cypresses, pigment, absinthe, epilepsy, reapers or
    sowers or gleaners,
but is, like color, as absolute and bodiless as the far horizon, the journey
    toward purity of vision.
Suppose the pattern of wind in the grass could signify deeper
    restlessness or the cries of land-locked gulls bespoke the democratic
    nature of our solitude.
Suppose the troubled clouds themselves were harbingers. Suppose the
    veil could be lifted.

James Wright, Richard Hugo, the Vanishing Forests of the Pacific Northwest

At least they died of smoke and age and not some awful, active form
of suicide. To keep sight of the forest for love of the suffering trees;
to damp the black or bitter ashes; not to surrender one's humanity
to callousness or grief: this is the hard part. There was much hardness
in their lives but no bitterness so terrible that what remained
seemed not worth having, no fatal poison in the pure American

wellspring. Where did they find such faith? How could America
retain its luster in eyes familiar with exile and war, the informal
inequalities of the factory floor? Why do the bleached remains
of Montana farms assume the character of barren cottonwood trees,
equal testament to the harshness of the local winter and the hardiness
of the will to endure, what Hollywood likes to call "the human

spirit," though why confine such a universal instinct to humanity?
Why believe it's we alone who suffer? How can the native American
ash and alder and Sitka spruce not possess some inkling of the harsh
truth when serpentine logging roads and clear-cut scars form
the totem shapes of grizzly paws on slopes bereft of trees,
when of the great, fog-shouldered forest so little still remains?

Scattered clouds above wheatfield.

Or does it? In Broadway stalls I've seen their work remaindered,
cut rate and still unsold, disregarded by the very people
they spent their lives extolling, and yet there is more in their poetry
than the ghost of the trees killed for paper. There is more to America
than wastefulness and greed and abuse, which are merely forms
of our inherent human weakness, manifestations of the hardship

we suffer when forced to choose for ourselves. Freedom is a hard
row to hoe, our cross to bear, individually and with whatever remnant
of communal will remains to us, whatever common vision yet informs
our deepest dreams and beliefs, the solitary will or the deeply human
dream of community, this central paradox, so typically American,
between the good of the wood and the rights of individual trees.

For me, they loom like redwoods or Douglas fir, the last big trees
of the endangered forest. The timbre of their voices, their wounded hearts
still large enough for sugar beets and four-door Buicks, all things American,
all things of simple dignity. Alone or gathered at the river, what remains
is the democratic song, their rich, vernacular empathy with the people,
a common thread of praise. Jim and Dick, in keeping with this form

I carve your informal names in a Western red cedar, totem-pole tree
of the original Americans, because it is sacred and strong of heart.
What thou lovest well remains distinctly, triumphantly human.

✳

The grizzly giant, Mariposa Grove,
California, 1866.

PHOTO: CARLETON WATKINS.

SHERMAN ALEXIE (1966–) ✳   *Alexie is a member of the Spokane/Coeur d'Alene Indian tribe and lives in Seattle.*
In addition to poetry, he writes fiction; he is the author of an acclaimed collection
of short stories, The Lone Ranger and Tonto Fist Fight in Heaven.[89]

The Business of Fancydancing

After driving all night, trying to reach
Arlee in time for the fancydance
finals, a case of empty
beer bottles shaking our foundations, we
stop at a liquor store, count out money,
and would believe in the promise

of any man with a twenty, a promise
thin and wrinkled in his hand, reach-
ing into the window of our car. Money
is an Indian Boy who can fancydance
from powwow to powwow. We
got our boy, Vernon WildShoe, to fill our empty

wallets and stomachs, to fill our empty
cooler. Vernon is like some promise
to pay the light bill, a credit card we
Indians get to use. When he reach-
es his hands up, feathers held high, in a dance
that makes old women speak English, the money

for first place belongs to us, all in cash, money
we tuck in our shoes, leaving our wallets empty
in case we pass out. At the modern dance,
where Indians dance white, a twenty is a promise
that can last all night long, a promise reach-
ing into back pockets of unfamiliar Levis. We

get Vernon there in time for the finals and we
watch him like he was dancing on money,
which he is, watch the young girls reach-
ing for him like he was Elvis in braids and an empty
tipi, like Vernon could make a promise
with every step he took, like a fancydance

could change their lives. We watch him dance
and he never talks. It's all a business we
understand. Every drum beat is a promise
note written in the dust, measured exactly. Money
is a tool, putty to fill all the empty
spaces, a ladder so we can reach

for more. A promise is just like money.
Something we can hold, in twenties, a dream we reach.
It's business, a fancydance to fill where it's empty.

Winters, Yvor: *"John Sutter"* from *Collected Poems* by Yvor Winters. Copyright © 1960. Reprinted by permission of New Directions.

NORTHWESTERN UNIVERSITY PRESS

Di Piero, W.S.: *"San Antonio de Padua"* and *"Ice Plant in Bloom"* from *Shadows Burning* by W.S. Di Piero. Reprinted by permission of Northwestern University Press.

OHIO UNIVERSITY PRESS / SWALLOW PRESS

Lewis, Janet: *"Awatobi," "A Grandmother Remembers,"* and *"Snail Garden"* from *Poems Old and New, 1918-1978* by Janet Lewis. Copyright © 1981.

Winters, Yvor: *"To The Holy Spirit"* from *Collected Poems* by Yvor Winters. Copyright © 1980. Reprinted by permission of The Ohio University Press / Swallow Press, Athens.

OPLER, MORRIS EDWARD

Opler, Morris Edward: *"Song For Girls' Puberty Rites"* from *An Apache Life Way: The Economic, Social, and Religious Institutions of the Chiricahua Indians* by Morris Edward Opler. Copyright © 1941. Reprinted by permission of the author.

ORTIZ, SIMON

Ortiz, Simon: *"A Story of How a Wall Stands"* and *"Canyon de Chelly"* are reprinted by permission of the author, Simon J. Ortiz. The poems are from *Woven Stone,* The University of Arizona Press, Tucson, Arizona. Copyright © 1992.

PENGUIN USA / VIKING PRESS

Lawrence, D.H.: *"Men in New Mexico"* from *The Complete Poems of D. H. Lawrence* by D.H. Lawrence. Copyright © 1964. Reprinted by permission of Penguin USA — Viking Press.

RANDOM HOUSE

Jeffers, Robinson: *"Rock and Hawk," "The Purse-Seine," "The Coast-Road,"* and *"The Vulture"* from *The Selected Poetry of Robinson Jeffers* by Robinson Jeffers. Copyright © 1959.

Snyder, Gary: *"Mid-August at Sourdough Mountain Lookout," "Piute creek,"* and *"I Went Into the Maverick Bar"* from *No Nature: New and Selected Poems* by Gary Snyder. Copyright © 1992. Reprinted by permission of Random House.

SHARLOT HALL HISTORICAL SOCIETY OF ARIZONA

Hall, Sharlot M.: *"Boot Hill"* and *"Poppies of Wickenburg"* from *Cactus and Pine* by Sharlot M. Hall. Copyright © 1989. Reprinted by permission of Sharlot Hall Historical Society of Arizona.

UNIVERSITY OF NEBRASKA PRESS

Neihardt, John: *"The Council of the Powder"* from *A Cycle of the West* by John Neihardt. Copyright © 1949. Reprinted by permission of The University of Nebraska Press.

UNIVERSITY OF NEW MEXICO PRESS

de Villagra, Gaspar Perez: *from "History of New Mexico"* from *Historia De La Nueva Mexico, 1610 Gaspar Perez de Villagra:* A Critical and Annotated Spanish / English Edition Translated and Edited by Miguel Encinias, Alfred Rodriguez, and Joseph P. Sanchez. Copyright © 1992. Reprinted by permission of The University of New Mexico Press.

UNIVERSITY OF OKLAHOMA PRESS

Cacamatzin: *"My Friends"* from *Pre-Columbian Literatures of Mexico* by Miguel Leon-Portilla. tr. from the Spanish by Miguel Leon-Portilla and Grace Lobanov. Copyright © 1969.

Nezahualocoyotl: *"Flower Songs"* from *Fifteen Poets of the Aztec World* by Miguel Leon-Portilla. Copyright © 1992.

Nahuatl: *"Song for the Festival of Tlaloc, the Rain God"* and *"Elegy"* from *Pre-Columbian Literatures of Mexico* by Miguel Leon-Portilla. tr. from the Spanish by Miguel Leon-Portilla and Grace Lobanov. Copyright ©1969. Reprinted by permission of The University of Oklahoma Press.

UNIVERSITY OF PITTSBURGH PRESS

Pape, Greg: *"Indian Ruins Along Rio de Flag"* and *"Making a Great Place Small"* from *Storm Pattern* by Greg Pape. Copyright © 1992.

Shelton, Richard: *"Because the Moon Comes"* is from *Whatever Became of Me* from *You Can't Have Everything* by Richard Shelton. Copyright © 1975. *"Sonora for Sale"* from *Selected Poems* by Richard Shelton. Copyright © 1982. Reprinted by permission of the University of Pittsburgh Press.

UNIVERSITY OF SOUTHERN CALIFORNIA: CENTRO CHICANO

Montoya, Jose: *"Faces at the First Farworkers Constitutional Convention"* from *Festival De Flor Y Canto: An Anthology of Chicano Literature* ed. by Alurista et al. Copyright © 1976. Reprinted by permission of El Centro Chicano — University of Southern California.

UNIVERSITY OF TEXAS PRESS

Anonymous: *"El Corrido de Gregorio Cotez"* from *With His Pistol In His Hand: A Border Ballad and Its Hero* by Americo Paredes. Copyright © 1971. Reprinted by permission of the University of Texas Press.

1 Miguel León-Portilla, *Fifteen Poets of the Aztec World* (Norman: University of Oklahoma Press, 1992).

2 Miguel León-Portilla, *Pre-Columbian Literatures of Mexico*, translated from the Spanish by Miguel León-Portilla and Grace Lobanov (Norman: University of Oklahoma Press, 1969).

3 Ibid.

4 Ibid..

5 Gaspar Pérez de Villagrá, *Historia de la Nueva México*, translated and edited by Miguel Encinias, Alfred Rodríguez, and Joseph P. Sánchez (Albuquerque: University of New Mexico Press, 1992).

6 Philip Morin Freneau, *Poems of Philip Freneau* (Philadelphia: F. Bailey, 1786).

7 William Cullen Bryant, *Poems* (New York: D. Appleton, 1866).

8 A. Thomas Trusky, editor, *Women Poets of the West: An Anthology, 1850–1950* (Boise, Idaho: Ahsahta Press, Boise State University, 1978).

9 Walt Whitman, *Complete Poems and Prose of Walt Whitman* (Philadelphia: Ferguson Brothers, 1888).

10 John Rollin Ridge (Yellow Bird), *Poems* (San Francisco: H. Payot, 1868).

11 Bret Harte, *The Complete Poetical Works of Bret Harte* (Boston: Houghton Mifflin, 1910).

12 Joaquin Miller, *The Complete Poetical Works of Joaquin Miller* (San Francisco: Whitaker and Ray, 1897).

13 Ina Coolbrith, *Songs from the Golden Gate* (Boston: Houghton Mifflin, 1907).

14 Frank Waters, *Book of the Hopi* (New York: Viking, 1963).

15 Matilda Coxe Stevenson, "The Zuni Indians: Their Mythology, Esoteric Fraternities, and Ceremonies," *23rd Annual Report of the Bureau of American Ethnology* (Washington, D.C.: Government Printing Office, 1904).

16 Herbert J. Spinden, *Songs of the Tewa* (New York: Exposition of Indian Tribal Arts, 1933).

17 Morris Edward Opler, *An Apache Life Way: The Economic, Social, and Religious Institutions of the Chiricahua Indians* (Chicago: University of Chicago Publications in Anthropology, Ethnological Series, 1941).

18 Frank Russell, "The Pima Indians," *26th Annual Report of the Bureau of American Ethnology* (Washington, D.C.: Government Printing Office, 1908).

19 Frances Densmore, *The Teton Sioux: Bureau of American Ethnology Bulletin 61* (Washington, D.C., 1918).

20 George Bird Grinnell, *The Fighting Cheyenne* (New York: Scribner's, 1915).

21   Franz Boas, *The Religion of the Kwakiutl Indians, Part II* (New York: Columbia University Press, 1930; New York: AMS Press, 1969); except "Warsong of the Kwakiutl," from Franz Boas, "Songs of the Kwakiutl Indians," *Internationales Archiv für Ethnographie*, 1896. The Kwakiutl songs included here have been adapted by the editor into poem form; the Boas versions are transcribed as fragmented prose.

22   Ruth Murray Underhill, *Singing for Power: The Song Magic of the Papago Indians of Southern Arizona* (Berkeley: University of California Press, 1938).

23   Frances Densmore, *Papago Music: Bureau of American Ethnology Bulletin 90* (Washington, D.C., 1929).

24   James Mooney, "The Ghost Dance Religion and the Sioux Outbreak of 1890," *14th Annual Report of the Bureau of Ethnography to the Smithsonian Institution, Part 2* (Washington, D.C.: Government Printing Office, 1896).

25   Washington Matthews, *The Night Chant: A Navaho Ceremony* (New York: AMS Press, 1978). First published in *Memoirs of the American Museum of Natural History*, 1902.

26   Edwin Markham, *The Man with the Hoe and Other Poems* (New York: Doubleday and McClure, 1899).

27   Mary Austin, *The American Rhythm* (New York: Harcourt, Brace, 1923).

28   Frank B. Linderman, *Bunch-Grass and Blue-Joint* (New York: Scribner's, 1921).

29   Sharlot M. Hall, *Cactus and Pine*, 3d edition (Prescott, Ariz.: Sharlot Hall Museum Press, 1989).

30   Willa Cather, *April Twilights and Other Poems* (New York: Knopf, 1933).

31   Witter Bynner, *Selected Poems* (New York: Farrar, Straus, Giroux, 1978).

32   John G. Neihardt, *A Cycle of the West* (New York: Macmillan, 1949).

33   Charles Badger Clark Jr., *Sun and Saddle Leather*, 5th edition (Boston: Gorham Press, 1920).

34   D. H. Lawrence, *The Complete Poems of D. H. Lawrence* (New York: Viking, 1964).

35   Hazel Hall, *Selected Poems* (Boise, Idaho: Ahsahta Press, Boise State University, 1980).

36   Stanley Vestal, *Fandango: Ballads of the Old West* (Boston: Houghton Mifflin, 1927).

37   Robinson Jeffers, *The Selected Poetry of Robinson Jeffers*, 9th edition (New York: Random House, 1959).

38   Gwendolen Haste, *Young Land* (New York: Coward-McCann, 1930).

39   Thomas Hornsby Ferril, "The Empire Sofa," from *High Passage* (New Haven: Yale University Press, 1926); "Blue-Stemmed Grass" and "Time of Mountains," from *Westering* (New Haven: Yale University Press, 1934).

40   Janet Lewis, *Poems Old and New, 1918–1978* (Athens, Ohio: Swallow Press, Ohio University Press, 1981).

41   Yvor Winters, *Collected Poems*, revised edition (Denver: Alan Swallow, 1960).

42   N. Howard Thorp, *Songs of the Cowboys* (Estancia, N.M.: News Print Shop, 1908).

43   Américo Paredes, *With His Pistol in His Hand: A Border Ballad and Its Hero* (Austin: University of Texas, 1971).

44   Theodore Roethke, *The Collected Poems of Theodore Roethke* (Garden City, N.Y.: Anchor Press/Doubleday, 1975).

45   Czeslaw Milosz, *The Collected Poems 1931–1987* (New York: Ecco Press, 1988).

46   May Swenson, *Nature: Poems Old and New* (Boston: Houghton Mifflin, 1994).

47   William Stafford, *Stories That Could Be True: New and Collected Poems* (New York: Harper and Row, 1977).

48   Thomas McGrath, *Letter to an Imaginary Friend, Parts I and II* (Chicago: Swallow Press, 1977).

49   Denise Levertov, "What It Could Be," from *Candles in Babylon* (New York: New Directions, 1982); "Settling," "Presence," and "Open Secret," from *Evening Train* (New York: New Directions, 1992).

50   Richard Hugo, *Making Certain It Goes On: The Collected Poems of Richard Hugo* (New York: W. W. Norton, 1983).

51   John Haines, *The Owl in the Mask of the Dreamer: Collected Poems* (St. Paul: Graywolf Press, 1993).

52   Carolyn Kizer, *Yin* (Brockport, N.Y.: BOA Editions, 1984).

53   David Wagoner, *Collected Poems, 1956–76* (Bloomington: Indiana University Press, 1976).

54   Allen Ginsberg, *Howl and Other Poems* (San Francisco: City Lights Books, 1980, 30th printing).

55   Philip Levine, "Waking in March," from *A Walk with Tom Jefferson* (New York: Knopf, 1988); "Snails," from *What Work Is* (New York: Knopf, 1991).

56   Adrienne Rich, *An Atlas of the Difficult World* (New York: W. W. Norton, 1991).

57   Gary Snyder, *No Nature: New and Selected Poems* (New York: Pantheon, 1992).

58   Alurista, editor, *Festival de Flor y Canto: An Anthology of Chicano Literature* (Los Angeles: University of Southern California Press, 1976).

59   Richard Shelton, "Sonora for Sale," from *Selected Poems, 1969–1981* (Pittsburgh: University of Pittsburgh Press, 1982); "Because the Moon Comes," from *Among the Stones* (Pittsburgh: Monument Press, 1973).

60   N. Scott Momaday, *In the Presence of the Sun: Stories and Poems, 1961–1991* (New York: St. Martin's Press, 1992).

61   George Keithley, *The Donner Party* (New York: Braziller, 1972).

62   Lucille Clifton, *Next* (Brockport, N.Y.: BOA Editions, 1987).

63   Lawson Fusao Inada, "From Our Album," from *Before the War: Poems as They Happened* (New York: William Morrow, 1971); "Concentration Constellation," from *Legends from Camp* (Minneapolis: Coffee House Press, 1992).

64   James Welch, *Riding the Earthboy 40* (New York: Harper and Row, 1975).

65   Simon Ortiz, *Woven Stone* (Tucson: University of Arizona Press, 1992)

66   Jon Anderson, *The Milky Way: Poems 1967–1982* (New York: Ecco Press, 1982).

67   Lorna Dee Cervantes, "Freeway 280," from *Emplumada* (Pittsburgh: University of Pittsburgh Press, 1981); "Colorado Blvd.," from *From the Cables of Genocide: Poems of Love and Hunger* (Houston: Arte Público Press, University of Houston, 1991).

68   Robert Hass, "Palo Alto: The Marshes," from *Field Guide* (New Haven: Yale University Press, 1973); "Spring Rain," from *Human Wishes* (New York: Ecco Press, 1989).

69   Pat Mora, in *Ms. Magazine*, January 1993.

70   Tess Gallagher, *Amplitude: New and Selected Poems* (St. Paul: Graywolf Press, 1987).

71   David Lee, *The Porcine Canticles* (Port Townsend, Wash.: Copper Canyon Press, 1984).

72   W. S. Di Piero, *Shadows Burning* (Chicago: Triquarterly Books, 1995).

73   Adrian C. Louis, *Fire Water World* (Albuquerque, N.M.: West End Press, 1989).

74   Linda Hogan, *The Book of Medicines* (Minneapolis: Coffee House Press, 1993).

75   Ai, *Sin* (Boston: Houghton Mifflin, 1986).

76   Greg Pape, *Storm Pattern* (Pittsburgh: University of Pittsburgh Press, 1992).

77   Juan Felipe Herrera, *Exiles of Desire* (Houston: Arte Público Press, University of Houston, 1985).

78   John Daniel, *All Things Touched by the Wind* (Anchorage, Alaska: Salmon Run Press, 1994).

79   Lynn Emanuel, *The Dig* (Urbana: University of Illinois Press, 1992).

80   James Galvin, *Lethal Frequencies* (Port Townsend, Wash.: Copper Canyon Press, 1995).

81   Paul Zarzyski, *The Make-Up of Ice* (Athens: University of Georgia Press, 1984).

82   Joy Harjo, *The Woman Who Fell from the Sky* (New York: W. W. Norton, 1994).

83   Jimmy Santiago Baca, *Black Mesa Poems* (New York: New Directions, 1989).

84   Gary Soto, *The Elements of San Joaquin* (Pittsburgh: University of Pittsburgh Press, 1977).

85   Ofelia Zepeda, *Ocean Power* (Tucson: University of Arizona Press, 1995).

86   Benjamin Alire Sáenz, *Calendar of Dust* (Seattle: Broken Moon Press, 1990).

87   Marilyn Chin, *The Phoenix Gone, the Terrace Empty* (Minneapolis: Milkweed Editions, 1994).

88   Campbell McGrath, *American Noise* (New York: Ecco Press, 1993).

89   Sherman Alexie, *The Business of Fancydancing* (Brooklyn, N.Y.: Hanging Loose Press, 1992).